THE GLORY STORY

SID ROTH

CHARISMA HOUSE

The Glory Story by Sid Roth
Published by Charisma House, an imprint of Charisma Media
1150 Greenwood Blvd., Lake Mary, Florida 32746

Cataloging-in-Publication Data is on file with the Library of Congress.
International Standard Book Number: 978-1-63641-622-9
E-book ISBN: 978-1-63641-623-6

01 2026
Printed in the United States of America

The author has made every effort to provide accurate accounts of events, but he acknowledges that others may have different recollections of these events.

This book could never have been written without the parents I had, the sister I have, and my wife and daughter. I see the hand of God on this book, which started before I even became a Jewish believer in Jesus. God is brilliant, and even with the world, the flesh, and the devil, God won in my life. And I pray this book will be the difference maker in your life!

—Sid Israel Roth

The glory of this latter house
will be greater than the former,
says the LORD of Hosts.

–HAGGAI 2:9

CONTENTS

FOREWORD

There are many believers who yearn to live in biblical times, especially the dawn of the faith—the days of the disciples, the apostles, Paul, Peter, the power of the Spirit, miracles, and the power of God's Glory. In view of that, one sign that we are living in biblical times and the Book of Acts is Sid Roth.

As were the first disciples and messengers of the gospel, Sid is a Jewish believer in Messiah—Yeshua, Jesus. That reality is still relatively rare in the world, but it was far more rare when Sid first came to the Lord. Like the very first Jewish believers and ministers of Messiah's love, Sid was and is a pioneer. They had no tradition to go on with regard to believing in Messiah. So for two thousand years, there was virtually no expression or tradition of Jewish people believing in Messiah.

So in that, Sid was a true pioneer, boldly proclaiming his faith in Messiah as a Jewish believer and doing so with no compromise, no hesitation, and no second thoughts. Like the apostle Paul, Sid has both a desire to touch all peoples and a burden to reach his own ancient people—his kinsmen, Israel—for Messiah. It was through that that I actually first heard of Sid.

It was back in the 1980s. I was a new Jewish believer. There were few other Jewish believers and few ministries to or of Jewish believers. I was in my car, heading to work, and I turned on the radio and heard, "This is Sid Roth! And I have a vision!" Here was a minister on the radio, Jewish, a strong believer in Messiah, full of enthusiasm and confidence in his faith, and demonstrating that belief in Messiah was not only an option for a Jewish person but was the most Jewish thing they could possibly do with their life. Sid's ministry was a constant encouragement to me and to countless other Jewish and non-Jewish believers.

And like the apostle Paul, he never stopped reaching out to his Jewish brethren for Messiah. His love and passion for his people have literally taken him across the world to share the love and power of Messiah with them. I can remember going on a journey to Communist China and there meeting with the underground church and a representative of the Chinese Jewish community. Among the things he told me was that a man named Sid Roth had come to China and reached out to him. Sid's passion for God's ancient people has never wavered or abated in all the years I've known him. He's as passionate now to reach them as he was when he first came to the Lord.

Another sign of the biblical times and the Book of Acts is the manifestation of the power of God, signs, wonders, and miracles. The apostles walked in the miraculous, ministered in the miraculous, and spread the gospel in the miraculous. In this too Sid is at the forefront and on the cutting edge. He has not only been open to the power and miracles of God, but he has yearned for them and sought them with all his heart.

This is one of the things that makes Sid and his ministry unique—he is always open to the supernatural moving of

God and wants to be wherever it manifests. He has opened up his ministry to this. And he has been a vessel himself in its manifestation. In ministering around the world, he has been used to bring healing and the power of God's Spirit even to people who came into his meetings not believing at all but went out filled with the Presence of God.

Biblical times were times of revelation and prophetic impartation. That is yet another thing Sid has in common with those first messengers of Messiah's love. Sid has a special gift for seeking out and finding where God is speaking—*now.* I can personally bear witness to this in what I saw of Sid in my own life and calling. People know me for the books I've written, starting with *The Harbinger.* But most people don't know Sid's role in it.

When I first shared the revelation that would become *The Harbinger* at my own congregation, Sid happened to get wind of it. He immediately called and asked me to come on his radio show. A couple of years later, I was led to share these revelations in a book. I told no one. But the very day that had been set for me to start getting the word out, I received a call from Sid Roth about the message of *The Harbinger.* He had no idea a book was coming, but he was just led by the Spirit to reach out to me and tell me he believed that this word had to get out to the world. And so I did his television show, and that was the vessel God used to get the message of *The Harbinger* out to the world. And Sid has been instrumental with every book I've written since, to get it out to the world.

The first believers in Messiah were filled with the Spirit and glory of God. And that is what I see in Sid. The Bible says we are to go from glory to glory. Most believers never apprehend what that means. But Sid Roth does. I don't know anyone who so much seeks the manifestation of God's Presence and glory as Sid does. And when I say that, I'm including people in their twenties. As I write this, Sid is in his mid-eighties, and yet his faith, his zeal, his passion, his excitement, and his wonder are as strong now as the day I met him decades ago. He has kept what the Bible tells us to keep, but most don't—that childlike wonder at the wonders of God.

I believe that is why God has so blessed him, and that is why he is going as strong, as excited, as powerful, and as young as ever.

And in that, I know that if Sid feels strongly enough about a revelation to share it in this book, it is well worth our time and attention.

Sid Roth—in his witness, his ministry, and his life—is a living Book of Acts and a model of how to walk and live in the wonder, the newness, the power, and the glory of God.

In sum, Sid Roth is truly an amazing man, vessel, and messenger of the Lord. And I count it as an honor to know him.

—Rabbi Jonathan Cahn
New York Times best-selling author
and prophetic voice

Introduction

THE MESSAGE THAT NEVER LEFT

THE OPPOSITION IS there so I can show you My Glory."

I believe this is a prophetic sentence. It has been stirring inside me for some time. I've heard it from prophetic friends. I've prayed over it. And now I've lived it.

I've just gone through the greatest miracle I have ever seen in my personal life, beyond my salvation, and it happened during the writing of this very book. That is not a coincidence. I want to tell you about it because it's not just my story. It's a window into the way God operates when your prophetic destiny is on the line.

In January 2026, I had been away with my wife on vacation in Georgia. Our plan was that I would return home on Sunday night, and my wife would come home the next night. So I was driving alone.

It was a five-plus-hour drive from Georgia to Charlotte, North Carolina. I was on Route 77, and the snow and ice in the Charlotte area were beyond anything I've ever seen since living here. The highway wasn't too bad, but the exits were horrible. I didn't realize this until I reached the exit near my home and hit a patch of ice.

What happened next was a situation I have never been in before—and one I pray you never face either. I totally lost control. I could not steer the car, so it was going by itself off the ramp. It was spinning around completely out of control. My first thought was, "I'm going to get hurt." My second thought was, "The car is going to be ruined."

But I'm going to tell you something: There are a few things I've been doing that had prepared me for this great miracle. I pray at least an hour a day, mostly in tongues. I read the Bible every day. I operate in what I call instant repentance—because I found the longer I wait, the more of a foothold the devil can get. So I instantly repent. I want to be as clean as I can in this life.

Most of the time on that five-hour drive, I had been praying in tongues. Now I was on the exit, spinning multiple times, unable to control the vehicle. And when the spinning stopped, I realized something: There could have been a car beside me. There could have been a car in front of me. I could have spun into someone. I could have gone off the ramp. But I didn't.

Instead, I landed on the side of the road, filled with snow and ice. I was stunned, but I was not hurt, and the car was not damaged. As grateful as I was for these things, it didn't take long to realize I was stuck in this snowbank. I could not go forward, and I could not go backward. I tried everything. I turned my wheels, and I rocked the car. But nothing worked.

I now faced a new problem: How long could I survive here in the dark, cold night if help did not come soon? Not knowing what else to do, I continued praying.

Suddenly, a pickup truck stopped right beside me, and then another pickup truck—coming from a different direction—stopped. The drivers of each pickup, two young men, got out. (I'd like to believe they were angels!) They saw I had a problem, and just like that, they hooked a chain to my car and pulled me free.

It could have been a very different outcome if they hadn't shown up. It was Sunday night with snow everywhere. I don't know whether I could have ever gotten anyone out there to help me. I told them they were part of a miracle.

As they drove off, I had a stunning thought. More than fifty years earlier, I had been alone in a car on another night, driving aimlessly, facing a despair so deep that I did not know whether I wanted to keep living. That night became a turning point in my life, and I share that story in detail in this book.

The parallel is not lost on me. Two nights. Two roads. Two moments when my life hung in the balance. Two moments when God intervened.

That is not a coincidence. That is destiny.

A Life Marked by Glory

For more than five decades, I have carried a single, unshakable conviction: God is real, supernatural, and active today. I didn't learn this through religion or tradition. I learned it through encounter.

When you encounter the living God, you are changed. Every time I share what God has done in my life, the same Presence of God returns. It does not return as memory or emotion but as a tangible Presence. It is the same Glory that transformed me from a deeply unhappy, frustrated, and lonely Jewish man into someone who knew, without a doubt, that Jesus—Yeshua—is Messiah. That certainty has never faded. It has never weakened. It has never left room to retreat.

Over the years, people have asked me why I talk so much about the Glory, why Israel and the Jewish people have always remained central to my heart and ministry, and why urgency seems to mark everything I do. The answer is simple: These aren't just my personal interests. They were—and still are—my assignments from God.

What others might call different seasons of my ministry are actually one story. At the center of that story is the Glory—the manifest Presence of God that transforms, protects, directs, and empowers.

A Story Still Unfolding

This book traces that journey. Part one tells the story of the supernatural encounter with God that changed everything. Part two reveals personal miracles I have rarely spoken about. Part three is my favorite because it is the prophetic reason my ministry exists. I explain why all of it matters now, especially for Israel and the nations.

For me, this isn't just history; it's destiny. Everything God has done through my life and ministry has been for such a time as this. And I believe my life is a prophetic blueprint of what God is about to do next.

When I walked away from that ice-covered ramp unharmed, I knew something with fresh clarity: God is not finished. You see, you and I have a book of life. Everything we are supposed to do is written there. Some of the things God tells me to do sound impossible unless God does them. But what I witnessed when those two men pulled me out of the snow proved to me once again: *God will do it.*

That night on the ice was meant to take me out, just like the night more than fifty years earlier was meant to destroy me. But God.

And that is why you are holding this book.

The opposition is increasing, but so is the Glory. I pray this book stirs your expectation into holy anticipation. What God has been doing in my life for more than fifty years has not been random, and it has not been just for me. It has been preparation—and I believe it will help prepare you as well.

When I look back, I can honestly say that it was never my plan. It was His.

And He's not finished yet.

PART I

THE FOUNDATION STORY

A Jewish Life Carrying a Question for God

Chapter 1

THERE MUST BE SOMETHING MORE

I WAS BORN INTO survival long before I understood the word.

My father was deeply Jewish—not in name only or through occasional holiday tradition but formed by a people's history that never really lets you go. My mother was born in Rochester, New York, and her father—my grandfather—was born in Belarus, in what was then the Soviet Union. Her family was a little more liberal. But my father was very religious. He was born in Poland, and had he not gotten out just in time, he would have been a statistic, a number, a story that ended before it ever had a chance to begin.

When I was growing up, my parents didn't sit me down and explain all that. In families like mine, children weren't given long, detailed conversations about past trauma. You lived. You moved forward. You worked hard. You stayed together. You survived.

There are things Jewish families do very well because we had to. We learned how to build a life on the other side of catastrophe. We learned how to keep going. We learned how to laugh again, how to make something beautiful even after the world tried to grind us into dust.

A Heavy Question for a Child

In many ways, I grew up in a traditional Orthodox Jewish family, attending synagogue, observing all the Jewish holidays, and celebrating my bar mitzvah at age thirteen. I believed there was a God, but the religious aspect of my Jewishness seemed abstract and full of hypocrisy.

In other ways, there was nothing traditional about my upbringing at all. I like to tell people that my parents were Jewish athletes—and their sport of choice was poker. They played poker often, and it wasn't a casual little hobby. It was their thing. There were nights when the game ran long. There were evenings when I was home alone. Long before *Home Alone* became a hit movie, I was living it.

I can still picture it. A quiet house. The feeling of waiting that doesn't have an end time. A six-year-old child imagining what might happen when the adults he needs aren't there.

And I remember doing something that only a child would do—something that seems almost silly from the outside but from the inside felt like the only control I had. I said the same words over and over:

I wish they'd come home.

I wish they'd come home.

I wish they'd come home.

I didn't say it once. I repeated it like a chant. As a child, I believed that if I said it enough times, it might happen.

Well, it didn't happen.

And then a question popped into my head. It wasn't a question a young Jewish boy was supposed to ask. In Jewish homes we don't discuss death. We emphasize life and being a good person. But the question came anyway: *What happens when you die?*

I remember thinking about it seriously. It was a strange question for a child to have, heavy and unsettling. In Judaism there is a belief in the afterlife, but our family had never talked about that. I didn't even know where someone would go to get an answer like that. If I had followed that question to its logical end with all I knew at the time, the conclusion would have been unbearable: You cease to exist.

So I did the only intelligent thing I could do. I blocked it from my mind. But questions like that don't disappear. They just go quiet for a time, and later they return with greater force.

Learning My Limits

Around that same time, my body introduced me to a different kind of vulnerability. I was diagnosed with Perthes disease.

Years later, my right hip was replaced. It's been more than thirty years, and it's still holding. Doctors told me the replacement would last only half that long. Maybe God gave me a new hip. What I *do* know is the impact that season had on my early life.

Physical limitations shape you. They affect how you see yourself. I was embarrassed that I didn't look like other kids. I hated people giving me extra attention because I used crutches and had a brace and one built-up shoe. Experiences like these teach you what it feels like to be different without anyone needing to say the word.

That experience followed me into school. I attended what was called a "health school" for children with disabilities. They brought everything down a notch, not because teachers were cruel but because they didn't want anyone to fall behind. They wanted everyone to stay with the program.

Something happens when people constantly lower the bar around you. If you aren't careful, you start believing you are the problem. For years, I thought I wasn't very intelligent because of those experiences. No one stood over me and insulted me, but when the pace is slower and the expectations are smaller—and you're surrounded by the message that this is the best you can do—something inside you begins to shrink.

But even in those years, a quiet resolve was taking shape. I didn't have the words for it at the time. I just knew I didn't like feeling limited. I didn't like feeling trapped inside a story someone else had written for me. I didn't know how to change it, but I knew I had to.

I didn't find the answers in religion. My Orthodox upbringing had provided structure, but it hadn't answered the deeper questions stirring inside me. I was proud of being a Jew, but I found the religion boring. God was just not relevant in my life.

I was bar mitzvahed at age thirteen, which in Jewish tradition marks a boy's passage into manhood. For me, it marked the point when I quietly decided I wasn't going to synagogue anymore, except for the high holidays.

When I got to college, a simple thought took hold of me. I decided I would apply myself fully—not casually. I wanted to see what would happen if I truly tried.

And something happened that surprised even me. I started making almost all A's. The reason was straightforward: If you do the work, you get the results. This lesson stayed with me, and it's one of the reasons God has used me for success. I never give up, and I work hard.

You would think that doing better in school would have answered the insecurity. You would think that proving to myself that I could perform would have resolved the question I had buried as a child. But it was still there.

What happens when you die?

Without an answer to that question, success is meaningless. It doesn't matter how much you accomplish if you don't know what your life is for.

Hungry for Something More

In college I wrote a song that I imagine every human being can relate to. I titled it "There Must Be Something More," and the words went like this:

> Because I work, eat, sleep, and that's
>   the way it goes,
> Because I work, eat, sleep, and that's
>   the way it goes,
> There must be something more than survival,
> More than routine.

I wasn't looking for religion or trying to become spiritual. I wasn't searching for a new identity or a new community. I was searching for meaning.

I didn't understand the hunger at that time. I only knew I was not satisfied. Something in me refused to accept a life defined by work, eat, sleep, and repeat. Something in me rejected the idea that the best you could do was survive, accumulate, age, and disappear.

The hunger kept pressing. There must be something more.

In a strange way, that sentence became a dividing line in my life. On one side was survival—heritage, identity, achievement, endurance. All important things. But none of them answered eternity.

I didn't know what the "more" was. I didn't know where to find it. I wasn't even sure if it existed.

So the question remained: *What happens when you die?*

If you can answer that with absolute truth, you can face anything. If you can't, then everything else becomes meaningless.

I still couldn't answer it. So I avoided it. I blocked it. I pushed it away.

Over time, that resistance turned into an inner insistence that said, "I am not here by accident. My life must mean something. This can't be all there is."

And that brings me to something I've learned after decades of walking with God. The hunger is not your enemy. It's God's mercy drawing you before you know His name.

There must be something more. That was my prayer before I knew how to pray. It was the seed of everything God would later do in my life.

Looking back, I can see that God was already moving, even when I wasn't aware of Him. He was shaping perseverance through physical pain and forming the resilience I would need later, when the story took turns I never would have chosen.

Even that childhood habit of repeating a wish over and over, as if persistence mattered, carried meaning. Because I would learn that persistence does matter—not in superstition but in faith.

I didn't understand that yet. All I knew was that hunger would not let me stay comfortable with a life reduced to waking up, going to work, eating, sleeping, and repeating the cycle until I disappeared.

I had no idea where that hunger would lead me. I didn't know it would take me into conflict and deception before it led me into freedom, that it would threaten relationships and reputations along the way. I didn't know it would challenge everything I thought I understood about what it meant to be Jewish.

But I can tell you this: I wouldn't trade the hunger for anything. Without it, I would have settled. I would have accepted survival as destiny and lived and died with the question unanswered. That would have been the real tragedy, never discovering what my life was truly for.

The Glory story begins here. You could almost say this is the story before the Glory. No miracles had happened yet. No supernatural encounters. Just a Jewish boy carrying a question and a growing hunger that refused to go away.

There must be something more.

Chapter 2

THE END OF MY SEARCH

Before my story became personal, it was historical. I come from a people who have survived against all odds, and I'll tell you something—that's not an accident. It is proof that God exists.

The Book of Esther records one of the most famous accounts of Jewish survival. Every year during the festival of Purim, we read this story to remember how the Jewish people survived Haman's plot to annihilate them.

The word *Purim* comes from the Hebrew word *pur*, which means lot, as in casting lots. When the devil attempted the genocide of the Jewish people, lots were cast to determine the date of this mass murder.

But Israel's future was not left to chance. God transformed the day chosen for destruction into a day of deliverance. He spared the Jewish people and destroyed those who plotted against them.

Generation after generation, our people have endured exile, persecution, attempted erasure, and hatred that defies logic.

The devil repeatedly tries to destroy the Jewish people for the same reason God spares the remnant. Why? I'll explain the answer more fully later in this book, but for now, just know that it's because God loves the Jewish people and will use them as end-time evangelists.

That same pattern marked my own life.

Looking back now, I can see that my life would eventually connect to that same purpose. But at the time, I had no idea.

Success Without Satisfaction

By the time I graduated from college, I had learned how to succeed in the real world. I knew how to apply myself, work hard, and push past limitations that once felt immovable. I graduated with honors and stepped directly into what, at that time, was considered one of the most prestigious professional environments in the world. I went to work for the largest stock brokerage firm on the planet: Merrill Lynch.

For a young Jewish man just out of college, this was more than a job. It was validation. It meant I had made it past the doubts that followed me from childhood. This job said I was sharp. It said I belonged.

Around that same time, I met a young woman named Joyce at a party. I call her Joy. She was a *shiksa*, a woman who wasn't born Jewish. She had been raised Baptist, but when I met her, she no longer believed her Christian faith and identified as an agnostic. We fell in love, she converted to Judaism for my parents, and we were married. Not long after, we had a daughter, whom we named Leigh.

I had been shaped by movies and the culture around me, and in my life the loudest teacher was television. TV advertising told and retold success stories until they felt like promises. The message was constant and reassuring: Wealth will bring you happiness, security, and respect.

So from the time of my first job as a paperboy to my career at Merrill Lynch, a single goal drove me—to become a millionaire by the age of thirty. I convinced myself that if I became a millionaire, I'd be the happiest person on earth.

For several years, it looked like I was on my way to reach that goal. I was young, ambitious, disciplined, and employed in a career many people envied.

But I blinked my eyes, and I was twenty-nine. Although I had a wonderful life, I started to feel like a failure because I hadn't yet made a million dollars.

I had done everything right to reach my goal, but deep inside, something was missing. I felt as though I had followed the map correctly, only to arrive at the wrong destination.

Looking for More in All the Wrong Places

With my dream of becoming a millionaire now slipping out of reach, I fell into despair. I consulted a fortune teller and asked him whether I should leave my wife. He told me I should, so I did. We didn't divorce, but we were separated.

I'm not proud of this decision. I was too young to call it a midlife crisis, but that's exactly what it was—a crisis of meaning, not circumstance.

"I got married early," I told myself. "I never did the bar scene. Maybe that's where the answer is." I knew something was missing. I was moving, but I couldn't get to where I wanted to go. I no longer thought about the future. Life was colorless, empty of meaning and excitement.

This went on for a year. Then one day, I walked into the same bar during the daytime that I visited in the evenings. At night, it looked like Hollywood—glamorous, alive, full of energy and promise. The music, lights, and seating arrangements suggested escape, excitement, and possibility.

During the day, it was the filthiest place I'd ever seen. The floors were sticky. The air was stale. The lighting was unforgiving. The illusion was gone.

I stood there for a long time. And something inside me went quietly sober as I thought, "There must be something more."

That moment forced me to face the truth that my hunger wasn't rooted in experience, freedom, or rebellion. It went deeper than that.

Still, I didn't know what to do with it. So I did what I had learned to do best: I kept moving. I decided to start my own company.

On the surface my life remained productive. Anyone looking in from the outside would have seen momentum. Inside, however, the unrest was intensifying.

The question I had tried to silence as a child returned with force. This time, it wasn't asking quietly anymore. It was demanding an answer.

All I knew was that the life I had built wasn't giving me the answers I was looking for. The things I had trusted to explain my life suddenly didn't explain much at all. And when that happens, you start listening to any voice that promises relief.

That is where my story was heading next.

Hooked on the Supernatural

From an early age, I was drawn to the supernatural. And because I had no spiritual discernment then, it was the wrong kind. New Age ideas, the occult, astrology, fortune-telling, handwriting analysis, reincarnation, hypnosis, and communicating with the dead all held a fascination for me, and that natural curiosity I had been born with turned these subjects into more than a passing interest.

As an adult, my attraction to these practices had become more practical. I was living in a world governed by prediction. The world of finance is driven by anticipation. You study trends, analyze patterns, interpret signals. You try to see what is coming before it arrives. In that world the future is currency.

So when one of my agents mentioned a relative who had taken a New Age meditation course—and opened themselves to a spirit that answered every question asked—it did not sound mystical or extreme.

I saw it as an advantage. If you can access reliable information about what comes next, you stop reacting and start leading. You gain leverage over uncertainty rather than being ruled by it.

So I signed up for the course. The introductory session promised that, by the end of the week, participants would know what others were thinking, be able to cure illnesses, and improve their finances. I was convinced that this was what I had been searching for. It felt like a can't-fail approach to all the acclaim and financial success I had been chasing.

As promised, by the end of the week, I had tapped into the supernatural in a new way. The instructor taught me how to lower my brain waves. When I was in this passive, hypnotic state, he told me to invite a "counselor"—a spirit guide—into my head. He said this counselor would answer any questions and perform any task asked of him.

At the time, I didn't know what I was dealing with. I didn't know that Scripture speaks directly about practices like these. I didn't know that the King James Version refers to such entities as familiar spirits (Lev. 19:31)—not because they are benevolent—they are evil—but because they generationally become *familiar*, attached, and influential in your life.

I took the course because I saw it as a way to sharpen my edge and access information others didn't have. In my mind it was no different from learning a new tool, something that would give me an edge. I didn't know that what I was inviting into my life had a name. All I knew was that it worked. And that made it even more dangerous.

On the last day of the course, the instructor tested my new power by giving me the name of a woman I didn't know. Then he asked me what was physically wrong with her. I asked my "counselor," and he showed me that this woman had breast cancer. "Could she have cancer of the breast?" I asked. My answer was correct.

This boosted my confidence. I gave my spirit guide a name, and since I had decided to open my own business, I said to this spirit almost casually, "Find me something."

Out of nowhere, a Gentile Christian businessman I had met casually said to me, "Sid, if you ever want to go into business for yourself, I'll give you a free office, secretary, and telephone." There was no pitch, no negotiation, no buildup—just provision.

I took him up on his offer. "Where do I sign?"

To me, this was confirmation that my new power worked. I saw it as proof that I had tapped into something real. My confidence in this spiritual power grew. "I have arrived!" I thought.

What I didn't know at the time was that I was listening to evil while the businessman was hearing from God. He and his associates were strong Christians who held prayer meetings at the office. God spoke to him and said, "You see that guy? He is so lost. He needs help."

I thought it was my power that had provided these things. But it was a much greater power. It was the power of God that set that up.

God was intervening in my life just in time. I didn't realize it yet, but I had crossed a threshold. And once you cross certain thresholds in the supernatural, curiosity turns into possession. The promise of power had done its work, and now the cost was about to become visible.

When the Supernatural Is Real but Not Safe

At first, nothing about my spirit guide felt threatening. You see, danger rarely announces itself at the beginning. It eases in quietly, waiting until you let your guard down.

In the early days, the experiences felt impressive. I would open a dictionary, point to a word, and the word answered a question I had been carrying internally. One day, I opened the dictionary again, pointed to several words, and strung them together. They formed a sentence: *Refrain from using the sinful book.*

I understand now that this was God intervening. I have since heard stories of people engaging with Ouija boards or other occult practices, only to hear a sudden interruption that points them toward repentance or salvation. And He continued to intervene in my life even as I misunderstood the source of the power I was engaging with.

That quiet intervention soon gave way to something more personal. One of the businessmen who rented me the office invited me to his prayer meeting. It felt so good trying to destroy his arguments and embarrass him.

One day, he stopped by my office and challenged the source of my supernatural powers: "Sid, did you know your own Jewish Bible condemns your involvement in the occult?"

He showed me from the Torah—Deuteronomy 18:10–12—and said, "The God of Abraham and Isaac and Jacob is not pleased with your involvement in mind control. He calls it an abomination. He condemns all New Age occult practices, and if God condemns these practices, guess where your supernatural power is coming from?"

He told me that the "counselor" who gave me information was a demon and very evil. Then he went on to tell me that Jesus was the Jewish Messiah that my Orthodox upbringing had carefully hidden from me.

His words frightened me enough that I began to search for answers. Could there be a devil, and could he be the source behind this power? Was my "counselor" a familiar spirit, and was it an abomination that I was consulting him? I sought advice from one of the top instructors of mind control in the country, but I was told there was no such thing as evil.

Up to that point, I had believed there was a God, and I was proud of being a Jew, but I had never taken the Bible as the literal Word of God. However, I decided that on the 1 percent chance the Bible really was from God, I had better stop consulting my "counselor" and start reading the Jewish Scriptures for myself.

I soon got the shock of my life. What that Christian businessman had said was true. No sooner did that thought form in my mind than the New Age spirit guide began cursing me from within. This "counselor" had a mind of its own, and it was from the pit of hell.

Until then, I believed I controlled this spirit, but now I knew that was not true. It had a strong power, and it was evil. I had to get rid of it. But there was no one I could go to for help.

And then things got even worse. I had been introduced to New Age concepts that went beyond mind control. One of them was astral projection—the belief that your spirit can leave your body and travel independently.

I was taught that during astral projection, there is no guarantee your body will return in time. That warning lodged itself in my mind, and the fear refused to leave.

Suddenly, the practices that had promised control began to rob me of it. Instead of clarity, I felt vulnerability. Instead of confidence, I felt exposed. I realized that I had been opening doors without understanding who or what might come through them.

Fear took away my sense of safety, and nighttime was when it hit me the hardest. I became afraid to sleep. Night after night, I lay awake, exhausted but alert. I was afraid that if I fell asleep, then my spirit would leave my body and be unable to find its way back—and that my body would be buried alive.

So I was sleep-deprived and separated from my family. Some might call me a first-class mess. I had reached the end of the line. Everyone has a breaking point, and I had reached mine.

A Life-Changing Encounter

As a young boy, I had a great fear of death because I thought that dying meant I would cease to exist. But now, for the first time in my life, the nothingness of death was starting to look better than my tortured existence. I didn't want to die, but life had become so hard that I didn't want to live either. Images from my past replayed over and over in my mind, exposing the darkness of the choices I had made.

This made the mental torture even worse, and one night, I considered jumping to my death from the balcony of my apartment. But I was afraid. If I did that, maybe I would land in hell, stuck with the awfulness that was myself for an unending forever.

Then I had a compulsion to go to a big bookstore I frequented.

As I entered the store, my feet took me automatically down the aisle to the New Age section. There, a book with a blue jacket leaped out at me: *The Bible, the Supernatural, and the Jews* by McCandlish Phillips.

I later realized this book was not in the right section of the bookstore. It should have been in the Christian section, but God had intervened, and someone had placed it in the New Age section right where I would see it. As I read the title, I thought, "Wow, if ever there was a book written just for me, this is it!"

I reached for it, and it fell open in my hands. So I began to read:

> If you would not thrust your hand into a snake pit, you should not permit yourself to be drawn into an involvement with one or another form of occultism, even in a tentative and experimental way, without knowing that it is possible for you to step over a threshold and past a door that will slam shut behind you as soon as you stand on the far side of it—slam shut so tight that nothing you can do can ever get that door open again so that you can get back out.[1]

Had the door already slammed shut on me because of my involvement with horoscopes, fortune-telling, and mind control? My heart was beating wildly as my eyes skipped through the pages a little further. There I read something even more terrifying:

> The door that can never be opened again slams shut faster on a Jew than on a non-Jew.[2]

The author went on to say that this is true because every Jew, whether he knows it or not, is in a covenant relationship with God. I felt beads of sweat popping out on my forehead.

My throat was on fire. The gooseflesh of fear enveloped my whole body, but I couldn't put the book down.

I shoved some money across the counter to the checkout clerk and dashed back to my car, the book tightly clenched under my arm. I wasn't even aware of driving to my apartment, just of suddenly arriving there, slamming out of the car, and dashing through the lobby and into my room, torn with warring desires. Part of me wanted to devour the book, to read every word; another part of me wanted to rip it to shreds and set it on fire—anything to get rid of it!

The page I opened to listed prominent Jews who had lost their lives because they had dabbled in the occult, opening the door to the supernatural through acid rock music, alcohol, marijuana, drugs, yoga, martial arts, meditation, channeling, séances, psychic healing, acupuncture, hypnotism, and mind expansion.

One name in particular caught my attention: Brian Epstein, someone I had idolized because he was the manager of the Beatles. A multimillionaire at thirty, Brian was a Jew. He had dabbled in the occult and died of a drug overdose three weeks before his thirty-third birthday. I shuddered, thinking how close I had come to following in his footsteps.

But I wasn't ready to die, and I certainly didn't want to go to hell.

My fortune teller couldn't help me. The mind control people couldn't help me. They said there was no such thing as evil. My rabbi? He'd probably send me to a psychiatrist who would lock me up and throw away the key. My mother, who had always been my protector, couldn't help me. She didn't know how to reach God either.

Panic-stricken, I ran to a jewelry store in the neighborhood and bought a *mezuzah* (a scroll with Hebrew verses from the Torah). I hastily hung it around my neck. Maybe that would help.

I telephoned Joy, my estranged wife. "Pray for me," I pleaded. "Pray like you've never prayed before! Pray for me! Ask God to help me. *Please* ask Him to help me. Ask Him to spare my life!" Joy had been a Baptist as a child, then became an agnostic in college—but I was desperate!

I let the phone fall from my hand, in the total agony of despair. I could feel the fear building in me, a tangible thing building toward a crescendo.

Feeling like a man under a death sentence, I put a Bible under my pillow, touched the mezuzah around my neck, and crawled—trembling—into bed. Lying there on my back, rigid with terror, I cried out, "Jesus, help!" It wasn't much of a prayer—only two words—but it came from a broken, empty man. I didn't want to pray to Jesus as a Jew, but He was my only lifeline left as a desperate, dying man.

The next thing I knew, it was morning, and something was different. The evil that had been inside me was gone. I knew it had to do with that prayer. My bedroom was flooded with the tangible Presence of God. Every cell in my body was invigorated with His life. The fear was gone. The spirit guide was gone, replaced by peace and what I can only describe as "liquid love." I had finally experienced what the New Age could never give me—the tangible Presence of God.

In that moment, I knew Jesus was responsible and that there was greater power in His name than in all the forces of darkness trying to destroy me. I also knew without a doubt that Jesus was the Messiah and that I had received eternal life. I repented and was instantly set free from all the demonic ties to the New Age and occult I had been involved in.

The atmosphere in the room felt thick, dense in a way I had never experienced before. I didn't have words for it at the time, but I know now that this was the Glory of God. In His Presence I went from feeling depressed and not knowing what to do to experiencing the greatest feeling I had ever felt.

I have never used drugs or abused alcohol, but I can say this plainly: Nothing compares to what I experienced that morning. No sensation, no escape, and no substitute even comes close. Whatever had been draining life from me no longer had authority. For the first time in a long time, I felt free.

Then suddenly, I heard a voice, and I knew it was God. There was no confusion about its source. The voice did not frighten me. It did not pressure me. It carried authority but not threat. It spoke clearly: "I hate divorce. Return to your wife and daughter."

I didn't know it at the time, but God was quoting the Jewish prophet Malachi. The command was precise, and I knew it was Him.

I didn't debate. I didn't negotiate. I didn't ask for time. I said, "Yes, Sir."

The restoration that followed was not instantaneous in every detail, but it was miraculous. My marriage was restored. My relationship with my daughter was restored.

And perhaps most remarkable of all, the peace of God surrounded me.

Day after day, I sensed it. The same Presence that had driven fear away was now with me all the time. And for the first time in my life, I knew I had found what I was searching for.

Chapter 3

MY STORY GOES PUBLIC

AT THE TIME, I thought rescue was the destination. My marriage had been healed. My mind had been restored. Fear no longer dominated my nights. The oppressive presence that had haunted me was gone. I expected life to slow down again, to become quiet and private. Instead, it accelerated.

I had been walking with God only a short time when my story moved beyond my living room walls. I didn't have language for everything that had happened to me. I hadn't even read the entire Bible. What I did have was an experience so decisive that it reordered my life from the inside out. And people noticed.

After my encounter, I told everyone who was breathing about Jesus! I told people in stores and people in restaurants. I even remember standing on a chair in a restaurant and preaching the gospel. I was radical! I knew God was real because He had rescued me. I knew the supernatural was real because I had encountered both its counterfeit and its truth. No one could talk me out of it.

That kind of knowing cannot be argued out of a person. It found its first public expression through the Full Gospel Business Men's Fellowship, an international network of businessmen with chapters around the world. Business leaders gathered to speak honestly about what God had done experientially in their lives. It was the perfect environment for me. I wasn't a pastor or preacher. I was a businessman with a story.

Even so, it's remarkable that I survived that first year. A Jewish believer in Jesus may not seem unusual today, but fifty years ago, it was rare. In fact, I was the first of my family, to my knowledge, in two thousand years—descended from the tribe of Judah—to believe in Jesus! It created tensions I had to learn to deal with in my Jewish family, and I'll share more about that in the next chapter.

My first speaking engagements were local: small gatherings, informal meetings, rooms filled with people who understood success but were still hungry for meaning. I spoke plainly. I didn't embellish or exaggerate. I told them exactly where I had messed up and exactly how God had intervened.

I talked about Deuteronomy 18:10–14, explaining that Scripture does not treat psychics, witchcraft, or fortune-telling as harmless curiosities. God calls them "abominations"! I shared what I had learned about this Scripture passage the hard way—that opening spiritual doors without God's authority leads not to insight but to bondage and even death.

People listened because I spoke as someone who had paid the price. I had been there. I had crossed those thresholds. I knew the fear that followed. And I had been rescued.

The Fellowship had chapters across the United States and in other nations. One invitation led to another. Before I fully grasped what was happening, I was traveling to cities I had never planned to visit and sharing my story with people I would never have met otherwise.

At this point, I was thirty-one years old. I had spent eight years in the stock business. I had spent roughly one year walking with Jesus.

I knew too well what God had rescued me from. I know how close I had come to losing everything. There was never any thought that I was special or that I deserved this. I simply knew God had done something in my life, and I had to tell people about it.

But not everyone was happy about my story.

When Private Faith Goes Public

On February 29, 1972, a major newspaper in Washington, DC, *The Washington Daily News*, ran a front-page article about a group they called "The White Collar Jesus Freaks." I was one of them.

The reporter was Jewish, and during the interview, I told him much more than was necessary because I was hoping he would come to believe in Jesus. I asked that my comments be off the record, and he promised they would be. But as I read the paper, it seemed like everything I told him not to print, he put in the article. I was stunned. I called and asked him, "Why did you do that? Why did you lie?"

His answer: "It was so good!"

I wasn't ashamed of believing in Yeshua. I was already talking about my encounter everywhere I went. But I was concerned about what this would do to my Jewish family. In the Jewish community I grew up in, I had never heard of anyone believing in Jesus. And my actions reflected on my parents and my entire family with shame.

You must understand how serious this was in the early 1970s. Today, people talk about Messianic Jews as if it's a familiar category. Back then, as I said, it was rare. There was no such label. No explanation made sense to the Jewish community. To believe in Yeshua wasn't seen as a spiritual choice—it was a betrayal.

For many Jewish parents, a son or daughter choosing to believe in Yeshua felt like losing that child altogether. It brought shame, grief, fear, and confusion. Some families treated it as a kind of mourning, even sitting shiva (the traditional seven-day Jewish mourning period for the dead). Others worried that their child had joined a cult. Almost all felt exposed.

For all these reasons, I had not wanted my testimony in the newspaper. But there it was—in black and white. The fallout was immediate. The phone calls came. The questions followed. The discomfort in my family was real.

I remember my Uncle Abe calling me and saying, "How could you do this to your father?" That question said it all. My father never confronted me directly, but I knew he was hurt and ashamed that men in his synagogue now knew my story. It wasn't because he didn't love me. It was because he didn't understand what had happened to me.

All that could have shut me up, but it didn't. And that proves how radical my encounter with Yeshua truly was. I would never have willingly placed myself at the center of that kind of rejection unless something real—something undeniable—had happened to me.

Like the apostle Paul, I was radically changed and ready to tell everyone about Jesus. I knew Him because I had encountered Him. That experience anchored me to something real.

Divine Intersections

Sometimes things happen in your life that seem like interruptions, distractions, or even inconveniences. But years later, you look back and see that God was doing something.

The newspaper article did something else I wasn't prepared for: My testimony became a headline. And that headline caught the attention of a television evangelist named Kathryn Kuhlman.

Kuhlman was widely known for her ministry from the 1940s through the 1970s. Her meetings were marked by healing and a deep reverence for the Presence of God. She spoke of the Holy Spirit as a real person who must be approached with humility and honor. She had the most authentic healing ministry I had ever seen. Even today, I have not seen such power as she operated in.

When she invited me to be a guest on her television program, *I Believe in Miracles*, I was surprised. I had been walking with Jesus for less than a year. I had barely begun to understand Scripture. And yet I was being invited into a space shaped by someone who understood the supernatural far better than I did.

After the interview, she offered to mentor me. If I relocated to Pittsburgh, she said she would train me.

I know now that it was an extraordinary offer. But at the time, I had no idea that the supernatural ministry of

Kathryn Kuhlman was so special. I thought miracles were common and all ministries operated like hers. So I turned her down!

That decision has followed me for years. I've often wondered what that season might have looked like if I had accepted. Today, I know that had she mentored me, my ministry would have been miracles for *all* people's salvation. Instead, God showed me that my ministry was miracles for *Jewish* salvation, to be the catalyst for greater Gentile salvation by going to the Jew first. I'll share more on this later.

So in place of having one formal mentor, I learned mostly by watching people around me. I saw people mishandle the supernatural and suffer the consequences. I saw what happens when someone moves in power without humility. I even saw ministries rise quickly and collapse just as fast. Those experiences taught me a lot.

One of my next television appearances was on a local secular television show in Baltimore. I thought I completely bombed it. I remember being asked a question and fumbling around, trying to find a Scripture passage I couldn't even locate. I felt awkward, unprepared, and frankly embarrassed. I walked away thinking, "Well, that was a disaster."

You might find it interesting to know that the two interview hosts were a Jewish man and a young woman named Oprah—yes, Oprah Winfrey was just starting her career. She kept saying to me, "You can't be Jewish and believe in Jesus."

Years later, a Jewish woman contacted me and told me her story. She said she had been watching that very program. She had just prayed a simple prayer: "God, if Yeshua is really the Messiah, show me just one Jewish person who believes in Him, and I will believe." The next moment, they introduced me on the show.

She told me that my appearance—what I thought was a failure—was the sign she had asked God for. And that night, she became a believer.

Her testimony made a deep impression on me. It taught me something I've never forgotten: God is not limited by our immaturity or by how little we know. He is looking for obedience, not expertise.

What I *did* know was simple: God is real. The supernatural is real. And the counterfeit is real too—and far more dangerous than most people realize. That message became my assignment.

I also knew that Jewish people were the underdogs, and I didn't know any believers in Jesus who boldly talked to Jewish people about Jesus, let alone on television!

More opportunities came—television, radio, speaking engagements, and travel. Everywhere I went, I shared my testimony.

Preserved for What Was Coming

Testimony is one of the most important things in a person's life. That's why I'm always sharing my testimony and have spent decades interviewing other people to capture their testimonies. You see the same Presence of God that caused them to become believers in Jesus jump onto the listener, and they get saved too!

I've shared my testimony so many times over the years that, if I'm honest, I've grown bored with sharing it. But I will never stop because I know the power released through testimony. This book is just another way I'm sharing that testimony, and I sincerely hope it inspires you to share yours too.

Your testimony could be simple or very supernatural, like mine. It doesn't matter. The same power released through a spectacular testimony is released through a simple one. That's why Revelation 12:11 says, "They overcame him by... the word of their testimony."

In fact, John 3:33 defines testimony as a seal of truth. The verse says, "He who has received His testimony has set his seal to this, that God is true" (NASB 1995). In biblical language a seal is legal confirmation. So John is saying that when someone hears the testimony of Yeshua and then believes it, they are sealing in the spirit realm that "God is true."

When I was first starting to travel and share my testimony, I didn't yet understand that. I was simply reacting to what had happened to me, not anticipating what would come from it. I just wanted to stay close to God and remain free from the things He had delivered me from. But God already had a plan that was much bigger than anything I could see at the time.

As I traveled and spoke, a pattern formed. People weren't interested only in my story. They were hungry for other stories like it. They wanted proof that the supernatural was still active. I began to see that my testimony was not meant to stand alone. It was a doorway, a reference point through which others could interpret their own experiences.

I didn't yet know what would eventually emerge. I didn't know there would be a global audience. But I knew this: What I carried was not personal. It was not simply instructional or cautionary. It was strategic. The salvation of Israel was central to what God had called me to do.

God had intervened not only for my own sake. He allowed me to experience the counterfeit so I could recognize it and help others understand the difference between what is real and what is not. He had allowed my rescue to be public so others could see that His mercy is real. I knew the truth.

That understanding helped me when people misunderstood me or criticized what I was saying. It gave me courage when others didn't approve. And it kept me steady when more opportunities began to come.

Publicly, by the mid-1970s, more doors were opening. I was sharing my testimony in more places. More people were hearing the message. And it was clear to me that God was the one making it happen.

But behind the scenes, things were unfolding more quietly. The people closest to me were still trying to understand what had happened to me and what my faith in Jesus meant. I was learning how to walk faithfully between two worlds.

Chapter 4

FINDING MESSIAH WITHOUT LOSING JEWISH IDENTITY

ONE OF THE most persistent misconceptions about my faith—one I still encounter nearly everywhere I go—is the assumption that believing in Yeshua required me to stop being Jewish. Nothing could be further from the truth. Let me explain.

As a new believer, when I first read about Paul's Damascus Road experience, something jumped out at me. His story felt strangely familiar. He was a Jewish man rooted in that identity. His encounter with Yeshua on the road to Damascus was a sudden, supernatural interruption.

In many ways, Paul's experience explained mine. It helped me understand what had happened to me. Paul did not stop being Jewish when he met Yeshua. In fact, he finally understood what it meant to be Jewish.

He did not abandon his people or his heritage after that encounter. Instead, he began telling everyone that the Messiah of Israel is alive. I understand that compulsion. Once you have encountered the risen Messiah, silence is no longer an option.

Paul carried that message into synagogues, marketplaces, and anywhere that God opened a door. And he paid a great personal price for it.

Some of his own people misunderstood him, and many Gentile believers failed to grasp Israel's ongoing role in God's plan. But he never denied who he was. He carried both realities. And in doing so, he became a messenger uniquely shaped to speak to both worlds.

In many ways, I have had to do the same.

I Was Born a Jew, and I'll Die a Jew

There's an understanding that many Jews grow up with, and I certainly did: "I was born a Jew, and I'll die a Jew." It's almost like an instinct we have from God. I still identify with that statement in every fiber of my being. Coming to believe in Jesus, known in Hebrew as Yeshua, did not change that. Just as a person does not stop being male or female when they come to faith, I did not stop being Jewish when I came to know Him.

When I encountered Yeshua, I did not feel as though I had crossed into a foreign religion or converted to something else. Instead, it felt as though something had finally been named. What had always been present, whispered in Scripture and carried through generations, suddenly came into focus. I did not lose my Jewish identity. I came to understand its fulfillment.

Messiah revealed the covenant rather than replacing it. Even when Jesus was dying on the cross, His title was written as "King of the Jews"—a declaration that the covenant was being fulfilled, not erased.

For me personally, believing in Yeshua brought peace to my Jewish identity. I did not have to choose between being Jewish and believing in Him. I did not have to walk away from my people to follow my Messiah. Instead of stepping away from covenant, I stepped more deeply into it.

With time, I came to realize why Jewish believers in Jesus often find themselves misunderstood. Within both Christian and Jewish communities, belief in Jesus is seen as a departure from Judaism. While the devil was deceiving the church leaders with anti-Semitic thoughts, he was also corrupting the authority of the Scriptures in Judaism. Both groups dug in and believed the big lie that you cannot be Jewish and believe in Jesus. And both views miss the heart of God.

If you are a Gentile Christian, you need to understand something clearly: Honoring Israel does not weaken your faith—it strengthens it. When you understand the Jewish roots of the gospel, your faith becomes more secure.

And if you are Jewish and wrestling with faith in Yeshua, please hear this without confusion or shame: Believing in Him does not erase who you are. You don't have to abandon your people, your history, or your identity. The Messiah of Israel does not cancel Jewishness—He fulfills it.

Much of the confusion about this comes from a misunderstanding about covenant. But God did not choose Israel to exclude the nations. He chose Israel to reach them.

When you see this, the Bible suddenly makes more sense. Your faith feels more solid. And you begin to see just how faithful God has been to keep His promises from generation to generation.

To be Jewish is not simply to belong to a people group or practice a set of traditions. It is to be bound to covenant. Jewish identity is inseparable from God's promises and His redemptive plan for the world.

God made a covenant with Abraham that did not expire with time or change with circumstance. He declared that as long as the sun, moon, and stars remain, there would be a physical Jewish people on the face of the earth (Jer. 31:35–36). That promise was not symbolic. It was literal. And the continued existence of the Jewish people is living proof that God keeps covenant.

When I read the Hebrew Scriptures after coming to know Yeshua, I did not see contradiction. I saw continuity. I saw a God who keeps His word across generations and does not abandon what He chooses.

This is where much of the church has struggled. Over time, some came to believe that God had replaced Israel instead of fulfilling His promises through the Messiah. This idea—commonly called replacement theology—has caused a great deal of damage. It has blinded many to the truth by distorting the Bible and has produced centuries of misunderstanding.

But God does not move on from the promises He makes.

When someone believes the church has replaced Israel, it does more than create confusion about the Bible. It distorts the character of God. Because if God could abandon the covenant He made with Israel, how could anyone be sure He won't abandon them too? The God revealed in Scripture keeps His promises. What He begins, He finishes.

Paul understood this clearly, which is why he wrote about Israel with trembling, not triumph. He warned Gentile believers against arrogance. He reminded them that they were grafted in, not self-generated. And he declared something unmistakable: "The gifts and calling of God are irrevocable" (Rom. 11:29).

Jewish identity was not rendered obsolete by Messiah. It remains part of God's ongoing story.

Living Between Two Worlds

As strongly as I knew who I was in Messiah, I also knew something else. In many churches I was too Jewish. And to many Jewish people, I was no longer Jewish at all.

Jewish believers in Yeshua have always made some people uncomfortable. That discomfort isn't really about personality or style. It's about what our lives represent.

When a Jewish person believes in Yeshua, he is doing more than making a personal confession of faith. His life becomes a living testimony that God has not changed His mind. Covenant still stands. Promises spoken thousands of years ago are still alive.

That kind of testimony unsettles people.

It challenges the idea that Israel has somehow faded out of God's plan. It confronts the belief that God has moved on. And it forces us to face something deeper about God's character: If God remains faithful to Israel through exile, rejection, and failure, then His faithfulness cannot depend on human performance.

When the church honors Israel, it honors Jesus Himself. The bottom line is that Jesus came to bring God's purposes to completion. He came as the fulfillment of the promises God made to Israel.

Once I saw that, the Bible opened up to me in a whole new way. History made sense. And the future no longer felt random. The logic became clear:

- If God has not replaced Israel, then Israel still matters.
- If Israel still matters, then God's promises are still unfolding.
- If those promises are still unfolding, then we are moving toward something—exactly as God planned from the beginning.
- Israel will be front and center stage in the last days. We are in the last days now.

There is no covenant between God and humanity that bypasses the Jewish people. Every saving, redemptive covenant God made in the Bible was either *with* Israel or *through* Israel. God chose to reveal Himself to the world through the Jewish people, and that was His decision, not man's.

In the traditional Jewish world where I grew up, the Messiah was something still expected, not someone already recognized. Jewish people are taught to look forward to His coming, to pray for it, and to believe that one day He will appear. But I didn't even know what the Messiah was, and no one around me believed that He had already come in the person of Yeshua.

It would have been easier for me to choose one side or the other. Many people do exactly that. They adapt to whichever group accepts them and hide the parts of themselves that make others uncomfortable. But God would not allow me to do that.

The gospel began in Jerusalem. And it will end where it began. There is no church without the root, no future without the covenant, and no "one new man" that Paul spoke of in Ephesians 2:14–16 unless both are honored the way God intended. Understanding this resolved my identity, but there was much, much more.

PART II

THE SUPERNATURAL STORY

How God Prepares Us Through Encounter

Chapter 5

MY FAMILY MEETS THE MESSIAH

When I encourage believers that this is God's appointed time to reach Israel—to reach the Jewish people with the gospel—many tell me they were taught that they should not evangelize a Jewish person. They believe the lie that they should never do that. Others tell me they've tried. They say, "Sid, I've shared Yeshua with Jewish people, but they're just not interested."

I understand why they feel that way. Because it can't be done by man's methods. And trust me, I'm an expert on how it *can't* be done. I have tried just about everything. But if it is God's time to reach Jewish people with the gospel as we prepare for the Greater Glory to manifest on the earth, then how will it take place?

God has given me a prophetic example for reaching the Jewish people through my father. His journey to accepting Yeshua was a long one.

When I first came to believe that Yeshua was my Messiah, the people closest to me assumed it was just another phase. My parents and my wife believed it was simply another one of "Sid's crazy pursuits"—something that would burn bright for a while and then fade, just like the others.

And given my history, I understood why they saw it that way. Remember, before I met the Messiah, I was searching everywhere. I was deeply interested in the supernatural, had no discernment, and pursued spiritual experiences with intensity. So when I came home talking about Jesus, it didn't register as the final truth to them. It sounded like the latest chapter in a long search.

My wife, Joy, was especially careful. We had a young child at the time, and her first concern was our family. She agreed to reunite with me because she wanted the marriage restored for the sake of our daughter. She was committed to the marriage, but she was also very clear: She was not going to follow me into this Jesus business, just as she hadn't followed me into the New Age. As far as she was concerned, this was my journey, not hers.

At the time, I didn't have much wisdom about how to walk this out.

When Words Didn't Work

It didn't take long for me to realize something that went against my instincts: Talking wasn't helping.

I'm an evangelist by nature. When something is real to me, I want to tell you about it—immediately and with conviction. At first, I tried to explain what happened to me. I tried to describe the encounter that had changed my life. I assumed that if I could just find the right words, the people I loved would see what I saw.

But with my family, words didn't move anything forward. They weren't hostile. They were hurt and unconvinced.

So I focused on my marriage and my daughter. I wasn't perfect, but I settled into the daily responsibility of loving the people God had entrusted to me. And something began to happen.

The people who assumed this was just another phase saw something they couldn't dismiss so easily. They noticed that I wasn't restless anymore. I wasn't searching for the next breakthrough. I wasn't moving on.

Something had shifted. And even though no one was ready to say it out loud yet, a different question was forming in their minds: *What if this is real?*

The Firstfruits

Of all the people in my life, Joy had the most at stake—and the most reason to be cautious.

Even though she had converted to Judaism to please my parents when we got married, she went to a Baptist church a few times, so I thought believing in Jesus would be easier for her than any of my Jewish family members. But that was not the case. She was still an agnostic. Her focus was on restoring our marriage for Leigh's sake.

I couldn't push her. I couldn't rush her. God knows how hard I tried.

Joy watched as the restlessness left me. She watched as the man she married—whose god had been money, whose search for more had led him away from their home, and whose life had spiraled into depression and even suicidal thoughts—became genuinely changed. Miracles are God's way of showing people that He's real, and for Joy, I suppose my changed life was the biggest miracle of all.

I had shown Joy the predictions about the Jewish people written thousands of years ago in the Scriptures. And she always said, "I have to believe the Bible is from God."

Then one day, when she was alone at home, she got to thinking about God and Jesus, and she said, "It's got to be true." Somehow, she just came to this conclusion that day. As she thought about God, she just knew, "It's all true." I believe the Holy Spirit came on her in that moment and moved her from thinking to knowing.

She didn't have a dramatic encounter like the one I experienced. She didn't point to a single defining moment. But she said something just as powerful: "I came to the conclusion that Jesus is the Messiah. I *know* it."

That was enough.

I often say Joy came in kicking and screaming, but when she finally crossed that line, it wasn't because of pressure or persuasion. It was because what she had been watching in my life for a year—and the undeniable, 100 percent accuracy of biblical prophecy—could no longer be explained any other way. Even the beauty of nature shouted God's vitality.

The marriage that the enemy tried to destroy, God restored. The relationship with my daughter, Leigh, that could have been lost, He restored. And then God did even more: My daughter went to a weekend Christian retreat where the pastor led her to the Lord. I was elated. God has been so good to me.

"Do You Have to Believe in *Him*?"

As the months passed, my parents could see I was becoming a real *mensch*, a person of integrity and honor. My mother, the great peacemaker, would say, "He's become such a good person."

My parents watched not only my wife and daughter become believers but also my sister, Shirley, my brother-in-law, Marc, and my nephews. When my sister lost her infant, Cheryl Ann, my parents and her Jewish husband observed her inner strength in dealing with this tragedy—a strength they had not seen in her before.

While my parents tolerated my beliefs, they were not quick to follow them. When I shared prophecies with my mom that proved Yeshua was the Jewish Messiah, it didn't faze her. She let me know she was grateful for the change in my life, but she was not ready to accept Jesus. "What would your father say?" Then she switched the subject. "Are you hungry? Can I get you something to eat?"

Over the years, whenever my mother was sick, I would pray for her, and God would heal her. One miracle even astounded me. My mother fell, and her knee was swollen, black and blue. It looked awful. I prayed, and instantly, it was restored to normal before our eyes!

This made her so proud of me. She would tell all her Jewish friends that if they were sick, her son would pray in Jesus' name, and God would heal them. Finally, as she observed the peace and fulfillment I had over many years, the Lord broke through, and she accepted Yeshua as her Messiah.

One by one, the people who mattered most to me encountered God for themselves—all except my father. So wherever I spoke, I asked people to pray for my father's salvation. My mother didn't want me to be disappointed. She would sigh and say, "Your father will never believe in Jesus!"

One time, when she said this, something beyond my control reared up from deep inside, and I said, "I know Dad will be a believer in Messiah!" From that point on, I said often, "I know my father will become a believer."

When my mother passed away, my father was still embarrassed and very hurt by my faith. He had been born in Poland and had seen anti-Semitism by so-called "Christians" firsthand. He told me that when he was a young boy, his father—my grandfather—would spit at a church as they walked past. My public witness for Yeshua brought him shame.

After my mother's funeral, my father had only one question: Was I going to say the *Kaddish* (prayers) for my mother in the synagogue every day for eleven months?

There was an ulterior motive behind his question. If I said the prayers for my mother, he could be assured that I would say them for him. And he believed that these prayers would somehow be his ticket into heaven, without punishment or delay. Since he knew I did not agree with this form of prayer, he wondered what my answer would be.

For a split second, I thought of the time commitment. It would require me to go to the synagogue every day. I thought of the endurance needed to sit through all the rituals and prayers in a language I didn't understand. I thought of the possible repercussions from those in the synagogue who knew of my outspoken faith in Jesus. But as quickly as these thoughts raced through my mind, I found myself agreeing to do it.

It had been years since I put on the *tefillin* (a small box with Scripture inside that is wrapped around one's head and arm, as commanded in Deuteronomy 6:8). A retired rabbi had to help me do it. After one service, I got into a conversation with the man who read the Torah reading that Saturday. It happened to be about the Jewish people walking through the Red Sea as though it were dry land.

As I discussed this with him, he looked at me with the most incredulous expression and said, "You don't really believe those stories, do you?"

Just as incredulous, I said, "You don't?"

When he told me he did not believe in God or life after death, I was curious why he came to the synagogue at all. He responded, "Because my friends are here. Because I like the food. And because it gives me something to do."

I always thought these men who *davened* (prayed) every day at the *minyan* (a gathering of ten or more Jewish men to pray) were the most holy Jews in the synagogue. But I found that many of the men I prayed with felt the same way as this man.

My father greatly appreciated my going to the synagogue every day to pray. And since I had not mentioned Jesus in a while, he asked, "Do you still believe in Him?"

I had been waiting for God's timing because every time I mentioned Jesus, my father would get angry. I told him that I believed in Jesus, and He was the reason I was going to the synagogue.

On another occasion, my father said men from the synagogue had told him that their sons would not have been so faithful to go to the synagogue every day. He would say to me, "Sidney, you're a wonderful son. You're as good as gold. But do you have to believe in *Him*?"

After that year, my dad had several close calls with death. Each time, I remember telling people, "Dad can't die. He hasn't received Yeshua yet."

Something Wrong with the Rabbi

After much prayer, one day I asked my father if I could read to him from one of our prophets—Isaiah. I told him Isaiah had written these words about eight hundred years before the Messiah came. He agreed, and I began reading Isaiah 53. (See appendix D.)

I hadn't gotten very far when he stopped me. When I asked him why, he accused me of reading from a Christian Bible. I showed him that it was published by the Hebrew Publishing Company, but that was not good enough. He said he would only accept a Bible from his Orthodox rabbi. "Hmm," I thought. "My father thinks Isaiah is speaking of Jesus."

So the next day, I called our family rabbi for an appointment. When I entered his office, he greeted me with a warm welcome and asked what he could do for me. I asked whether he would give me a Bible and inscribe something personal to me. He gladly complied, writing some kind words to me on the inside cover. I thanked him and left quickly. I could not wait to show this powerful gift to my father.

When I arrived, I confidently displayed the inscription to my dad and made sure he read it. Then I began to read the same passage from Isaiah 53. Now he had only two choices.

Either he had to agree that Jesus was the Messiah, or he had to think something was wrong with the rabbi.

To my shock, he said, "I've always thought there was something wrong with that rabbi." And then he told me how he once saw the rabbi eating out in a restaurant on Yom Kippur—the day of fasting.

I smile when I think about that moment because I recognize what was happening. He wasn't rejecting the Scripture. He was pushing back against what it meant.

Heaven Must Be a Wonderful Place

Years later, I got the call from my sister that my father was dying. Shirley and her husband, Marc, had been believers in Yeshua almost as long as I had. "It looks bad," she told me. "You'd better come."

Something unusual had happened to me a week earlier. A strong Presence of God had been on me constantly for several days. It was the same tangible Presence as when Jesus first became real to me years earlier. It was the Glory. This time, it stayed with me twenty-four hours a day, and it was getting stronger. I didn't know the reason for it, but I was grateful.

When I arrived, I met my sister at the hospital, and we went straight to the ICU. My dad was eighty-three and had prostate cancer. Since the cancer had invaded his bones, we knew he could die at any moment. His voice was so weak that he could barely speak above a whisper.

I said, "Dad, do you remember how Mom always said, 'Heaven must be a wonderful place'? Don't you want to be with her? And with me and Shirley and our children? Do you want to make Yeshua your Messiah and Lord?"

He replied, "Yes," and I got ready to pray with him.

But my sister Shirley said, "Sid, I didn't hear him."

I responded, "I heard him." I knew it had been a whisper, but that was good enough for me.

Shirley felt otherwise. She put her hands on her hips and said, "I'm not sure." She turned to our father and said, "Dad, do you want to make Yeshua your Messiah and Lord?"

My father got his old spunk back and belted out, "Yes!"

With that, Shirley jumped up and down and screamed, "Thank You, Yeshua! Thank You!" My sister was a refined schoolteacher, so this outburst was totally out of character for her. Besides, everyone is supposed to remain very quiet in the ICU.

I tried to calm her down, but to no avail. She said, "I promised the Lord I would jump for joy when Dad was saved!"

After we prayed with him, my father went to heaven the next day.

A Lifetime of Surrender

I am a very thankful person. Every member of my immediate Jewish family believes in Yeshua, including the younger generations who've been born since this story began. My sister Shirley and her husband, Marc, now have three sons who are believers in Jesus. My daughter, Leigh, is a Jewish believer in Yeshua, and she blessed Joy and me with three granddaughters. My first granddaughter is named Olivia because she is the fruit of the Jew and Gentile grafted into the olive tree. I speak and text with my granddaughters weekly. Joy and I have celebrated over sixty years of marriage.

It has been more than fifty years since I was set free. I am a blessed man.

Seeing my own Jewish family come to know Yeshua as Messiah blessed me beyond measure. These are the people I love most in the world. I watched God open their eyes. I watched Him answer prayers I had carried for years. Once you witness His faithfulness like this, you understand that God wants to reveal Himself. He confirms His Word. He keeps His promises.

From that point on, I understood something clearly: If you follow the God of Israel, you must expect the supernatural.

Chapter 6

WHY THE SUPERNATURAL WAS NEVER OPTIONAL

I OFTEN ASK MYSELF how I went from a brand-new believer to more than fifty-five years of following God—still in full-time ministry at eighty-five. The answer is simple, and it has never changed: I encountered the living God. I had experiential knowledge of God, and He took me on the most supernatural journey I could have ever imagined.

Scripture says that the Jews require a sign (1 Cor. 1:22). Jewish people are interested in the supernatural. I have observed that a very high percentage of the leaders and followers in the New Age and other cult and occult groups are the Jewish people! When Christians are ill-equipped to demonstrate authentic miracles of God, Satan's counterfeit power will gladly take their place. But authentic signs and miracles prove the reality of God and open the door to proclaiming why Jesus is the Jewish Messiah.

I did not grow up resistant to God. I grew up unfamiliar with His Presence and reality. Although I attended an Orthodox synagogue, I knew very little of the Scriptures.

I had spent most of my time in the synagogue reading the prayer book and learning our traditions.

If you had asked me whether I believed in God, I would have said yes, but I had never really thought about it. God was just not relevant.

What I did not know—what few of us had ever been shown—was that the God of Israel still spoke, still healed, still intervened, and still made Himself known. And unfortunately, most Christians don't have this experiential knowledge of God either.

Many believers have been taught that expecting God to act is risky. That it can disappoint. That it can attract extremes.

But Scripture doesn't treat God's power as an advanced option for unusual people. It treats it as normal. The gospel was never meant to be carried by information alone. It was meant to be carried by the Spirit of God.

In the world we live in now, people are hungry for the supernatural. Spiritual hunger will be answered by something. If the church does not demonstrate a living God, people will not stop seeking power—they will just find it in the wrong places.

So I'm calling you to stop building your life around what feels manageable and start making room for a God who still confirms His Word. The Book of Acts shows us what normal looks like. It's time to be normal!

I have watched many well-meaning Christians reason with Jewish people. They debated Scripture, defended doctrine, and tried to explain why Jesus is the Messiah. Almost without exception, they walked away frustrated. Early on, I tried all these methods too. But argument was never God's chosen doorway into Jewish hearts. Encounter was. Then they are open to the scriptural evidence.

As you've read in this book, when God intervened in my own life, He did not argue with me. He did not negotiate. He did not wait for me to reason my way toward belief. He spoke, and His Presence followed His voice. I went to sleep broken, confused, and afraid. I woke up immersed in a Presence so real and overwhelming that it silenced every unanswered question I had carried since childhood. I woke up with true joy and contentment.

From that moment on, I knew something I could never unknow.

Once you have encountered the living God, persuasion becomes unnecessary. You don't defend what you have experienced. You don't debate what has already changed you. You simply live from it.

I did not set out to convince people. I set out to introduce them—to invite them into the same encounter that had rescued me. I wasn't trying to win debates. I was trying to remove veils. Scripture had already made it clear: The veil does not lift through reasoning; it lifts through revelation (2 Cor. 3:14–16). The Glory or Presence of God wins all arguments.

Paul didn't argue his way into faith. He encountered Jesus on the road to Damascus. The prophets didn't persuade Israel through logic alone. God confirmed His word with power. Healing, deliverance, and miracles were never accessories to the message. They *were* the message. They were God's way of saying, "I am here."

God Orchestrates Visibility

As I write this book, I'm not only still in full-time active ministry, but I'm more active now than at any other point in my life. I am deeply grateful for the deliverance I received because once God rescued me, nothing could discourage me from preaching the gospel.

Wherever I went, I left no one without a witness, and I mean a strong witness. As a young man in business, I knew how to close a sale. When I came to know God, I understood how to "close the sale" there as well—by praying with people and inviting them to encounter Him for themselves.

It never occurred to me that someone might not be healed. My reference point was the Bible. The New Testament says that Yeshua healed them all, and I took that literally. I wanted to lead everyone to the Lord. Every week, I was speaking somewhere, and news articles were being written about what was happening.

After the article in *The Washington Daily News* appeared in 1972, a woman named Sandra Sheshkin invited me to go to the Hebrew Christian Alliance. I agreed to go, and for the first time, I found myself connecting with other Jewish believers in Yeshua. I became friends with a whole group of Jewish believers and also met many charismatics, who were mostly Gentiles.

Just as I joined the group, it changed its name to the Messianic Jewish Alliance. I soon became president of the Washington, DC, chapter. We had a picnic, and one of the members who came was from Chicago. He told me they had a Messianic synagogue there, and he recommended starting one in our area.

When I first heard about the idea of a Messianic synagogue, I thought, "That doesn't sound like a good idea. Why do we need that?"

Even though I was unconvinced, we put it to a vote, and the majority of the members voted to start a Messianic synagogue. So just like that, we started Beth Messiah congregation in Rockville, Maryland, as a community for Jewish people who believed in Jesus.

Most of us knew almost nothing. Many in our leadership were new believers. We had no rabbi, so we rotated our elders to speak. I was what you might call a figurehead, but I didn't call myself a rabbi or anything. I barely knew the Bible.

There were about one hundred members of the Messianic Jewish Alliance in Washington, DC, and about fifteen would attend the meetings. That was our core group. And every week, people would come forward because there was a genuine move of God's Spirit.

Beth Messiah became one of the premier congregations in the United States and, I believe, in the world. It became a role model. We intentionally reached Jewish people when very few others did.

In our early years during the seventies, we reacted out of immaturity. In our desire to honor our Jewish identity, we overcorrected. We began equating Jewishness with outward forms, borrowing from traditional synagogue expressions of worship and presentation. We believed that appearing more Jewish would make us more acceptable to the Jewish community.

It did not.

At the same time, we were misunderstood and resisted by parts of the Gentile church. Many Christians called us a cult. Caught between rejection and insecurity, we tried even harder to prove who we were.

We did not reach many Jewish people. And unintentionally, as we tried to reach the Jewish people, we made Gentile believers who loved us feel like second-class citizens. Our intentions were sincere, but our approach was unbiblical. That is something I regret.

Eventually, we realized we needed someone who actually knew something. We brought in a Messianic Jewish rabbi named Manny Brotman, a pioneer in Jewish evangelism who had devoted his life to sharing Messiah with Jewish people. (Sandra, who had first invited me to the alliance, eventually became Manny's wife.) I shared office space with him, and I learned from him.

One day, a man walked into our office and said, "Manny, I want you to do a radio show on our top station." Manny said yes—and then turned to me and said, "Sid, you'll be the announcer." I didn't want to be behind the microphone. I wanted to be the businessman making the person behind the mic successful. I was terrified.

Manny sent me home to write a script. I did, and that is how I became the announcer. And whenever Manny couldn't do the show, he believed I was the best person to step in. I fought it at first but discovered I was good at it.

Soon after, I started a secular radio show, one of the great thrills of my life. It was on the secular radio station that played religious programs on Sunday, and it became the top Jewish radio program on Sunday mornings in the Washington, DC, area. There was a reason God directed me to be on this secular radio station, at that day and time: I bought the half hour immediately following *The Max Resnick Show.* Max, a traditional Jewish man, had built a strong Jewish audience and told them about good Jewish things, and then I came on after his show and told them about Jesus.

Later, I went to New York City and hosted a live call-in show on one of the top secular stations, openly proving that Jesus was the Messiah. Once a week, as I traveled to New York, I felt like I was invading the devil's territory.

I started a second Messianic synagogue in Brighton Beach, a neighborhood in southern Brooklyn, where one hundred thousand Russian Jews lived within a ten-block radius. It's like going to Russia when you go there, and so we invaded with the gospel!

For one of our meetings, some Orthodox Jews showed up and formed a blockade to stop people from attending. They were starting to fight, so the police were called in. They had to intervene to stop the Orthodox Jews from threatening the Russian Jews who wanted to come inside.

We're all wired differently. A lot of people would never want to be involved with something like that, but I loved it.

God had planted a love in my heart for the Russian Jews. It all started when I made a trip with Messianic Jewish leader Jonathan Bernis to what was then the Soviet Union and saw how open the Soviet Jews were to the gospel.

Jonathan had simply knocked on my door one day, and we became fast friends. One day, he said to me, "I feel God is calling me to Russia. Would you go with me to Moscow and St. Petersburg and kind of explore it with me?" I agreed.

We rented a big hall and advertised for a Jewish meeting. It was Jonathan's meeting, and I just went to give him support, so to speak. But then he said, "OK, Sid, you speak one night, and I'll speak one night." So we rotated.

Jonathan, who ultimately stayed in the former Soviet Union for several years, would organize Jewish music festivals because they appealed to Jewish people. He'd fill an auditorium, have the Jewish music festival as advertised, give his testimony, and people would run forward. I mean, the first time I saw it, I couldn't believe it. They didn't walk forward to be saved—they *ran.*

So Jonathan would do one night based on the music festival and sharing his testimony. I would do the next night based on the music festival and sharing my testimony. When I would speak, I got the same results, except my attention grabber was miracles.

I was grateful that God did not call me to live in the Soviet Union like Jonathan. Times were very hard there, and you had to stand in long lines for food. I was very appreciative to return to America and go on to hold my own series of "Lectures on the Supernatural" while Jonathan remained in the Soviet Union.

After I returned to the States, I got a phone call from a Russian Jewish believer who lived in Brighton Beach. She told me how many Jewish people lived in that ten-block radius and said, "I'll get them to show up if you'll come and share your testimony."

I agreed, and when I arrived, her entire apartment was jam-packed with Russian Jews: little ones, big ones, old ones, young ones, tall ones, short ones. They didn't even have chairs for all of them. I had never seen so many Jewish people in one place before.

I shared the gospel, and every single one of them received the Lord. Even though I had been an evangelist for many years by that time, I had never had that happen before. It was amazing.

And when they received the Lord, words of knowledge and miracles started to flow. One woman, so hobbled by arthritis that she could barely even get to the meeting, was totally healed and walked all the way home—ten blocks! Word spread that a Jewish man prayed for the sick in the name of Jesus, and people were healed. From the very beginning, God orchestrated all this.

As a result of that experience, I said, "I've got to start a ministry to reach Jewish people in Brighton Beach." I found out that many people before me had seen what I was seeing and had gone to Brighton Beach and tried to start ministries, but the devil had knocked every one of them out. I mean, horrible situations had occurred.

Still, I persevered. I went to every church in Brighton Beach I could find and asked whether I could use their building for a Bible study. Every church turned me down. Then I went to the movie theater, and they turned me down. Then I went to all the schools, and they turned me down.

Here I was with all these Jewish people who were open to the gospel, and I couldn't find a location!

Finally, when I was about to give up, I got a phone call from the Board of Education, and they said we could meet in one of the public schools. We ran advertisements about the meetings in Russian-language newspapers and began holding them. I never could have anticipated the results we experienced. In the first week, twenty-three people came to the Bible study, and all twenty-three came to the Lord!

Every week, we ran ads and Jewish people kept coming to accept the Lord. From there, we continued to grow, holding services in both English and Russian, and eventually formed a Messianic synagogue for the Russian Jews in that community.

God Always Does More Than We Expect

Zechariah 4:6 says, "Not by might or by power, but by My Spirit, says the Lord of Hosts." And that's what I experienced. There was such an anointing on those services that I often thought, "I could just read the telephone book and people would come forward to receive Jesus!"

Wherever I went, I spoke. And wherever I spoke, I prayed. It wasn't enough for me to share information about God; I wanted people to know Him. I wanted them to encounter the same Presence that had rescued me when I reached the end of myself. And God showed up every time!

One thing led to another, and before I knew it, we were planning something bigger than I had ever imagined.

Messianic congregations like the one I helped pioneer were now spreading to all the major cities across the United

States and around the world. I didn't have a clue we were making spiritual history when I mobilized the largest gathering of Messianic Jews in Israel in over 1,900 years. It was called Shavuot '88. That was almost forty years ago on Pentecost (Shavuot). The historical part was not in booking almost an entire El Al jet, jam-packed with 476 mostly Messianic Jews from America, nor the 500-plus who joined us from Israel at our conference hotel in Jerusalem. Rather, it was what happened thirty years later at that very hotel at almost the same time.

We chose that location because it was the only Jewish-owned hotel in Jerusalem that allowed us to use a microphone, given rabbinic restrictions on Shavuot. One of our opening speakers prophesied that fire from heaven would come in that building, saying, "Everyone who asks receives." The fire of God did come thirty years later!

Only the fire of God could have placed a US president in office who would have the nerve to move the US embassy to Jerusalem despite intense pressure from Arab oil interests and threats from terrorist organizations.

And guess which property the embassy purchased? The hotel where we staged our conference.

And guess when they opened the embassy? Just days before Shavuot 2018. The intense prayer by so many Messianic Jews thirty years prior literally brought the fire from heaven and, against all odds, birthed our US embassy in Jerusalem!

I have to tell you something about myself: My expectations are always higher than results. But that conference exceeded every expectation I had. We also held what I believe was the first and possibly largest Messianic Shabbat service in history. Over forty years ago, R. W. Schambach—a faith healing evangelist known for holding massive tent revivals (similar to Oral Roberts, T. L. Osborn, and other healing evangelists of the 1940s and 1950s)—gave us the use of his great gospel tent, which could hold five thousand people. We advertised a Messianic Shabbat service in Coney Island, NY, and the tent was packed with both Jewish people and Gentiles. Multitudes came to the Lord. Multitudes were healed.

As God continued to confirm His Word, doors opened that I never sought and never could have orchestrated. I became a regular guest on programs like *The 700 Club* and *PTL*. One day, Jim Bakker's producer asked me to host *The PTL Club* while Jim was on vacation. I was still a young believer and had no idea what I was doing—but suddenly, I was hosting the show.

We did something they had never done before: a Messianic Jewish *PTL Club*. Afterward, some rabbis protested, and Jim promised them it would never happen again. But God had already marked the moment.

What struck me most in all these endeavors was the consistency. God was confirming His Word in private conversations and on public platforms, in small gatherings and massive rooms, across cultures and continents. And once He does that, nothing stays small for long.

Chapter 7

TAKING THE SUPERNATURAL TO THE AIRWAVES

IF I HAD the choice of any generation in all history to live in, I would choose this one. We have seen more Bible prophecy fulfilled than any generation that has ever walked the earth, with the sole exception of the prophecies Yeshua fulfilled to prove He is the Messiah.

If I had told you early on what I thought my role would be after coming to faith, it would not have sounded anything like what unfolded. My calling was simple. I wanted my own Jewish people to know that Yeshua is the Messiah. That has always been my heart.

God had other plans.

Over the years, He began expanding the reach of the message in ways I never could have planned. One small step would open the door to another. And before long, what started as a simple desire to share the gospel began reaching people all over the world.

Looking back now, I can see that God was not just reaching the Jewish people. He was using media to reach anyone who was hungry to know that the God of the Bible is real.

Small Beginnings

The prophet Zechariah's admonition to "not despise these small beginnings, for the Lord rejoices to see the work begin" (Zech. 4:10, NLT) certainly applies to my life. It's funny how most of the things in my ministry started that way.

Long before Messianic Vision was incorporated in 1977, I began recording interviews for radio on a small, portable, battery-operated cassette recorder. When we were able to upgrade, I contracted a recording studio in the country. I would drive my guests two hours round-trip to record and edit their shows professionally. The roads had turns almost every quarter mile through mostly wooded, undeveloped areas.

One early guest I will never forget is the late Dr. Derek Prince, who, in my opinion, was one of the greatest end-time Bible teachers of his generation. As I drove Derek through those twisting country roads, he said in his strong British accent, very sternly, "Are you kidnapping me?"

We both laughed hysterically, although I was never sure whether he actually thought he was being kidnapped—at least for the first ten minutes!

At the time, I had no idea what God was building. To me, it was just one interview at a time. One conversation at a time. One person at a time, sharing about the reality of God.

But over time, those interviews began reaching more and more people.

TELEVISION EXPANDS THE CALL

Then one day, a member of my staff, Janie DuVall, told me I should do television. I said no, but she kept insisting. Out of the blue, a friend in Canada gave me $25,000 to do a television show. She had no idea I was thinking about this. She was even bolder—she gave the $25,000 to a television network in Canada. I had now been given the idea, the money, and even the studio.

But it got even more supernatural. I had a Jewish friend named Warren Marcus. He had worked as a producer for *The 700 Club*. He won awards for his outstanding productions. But his heart was for Jewish evangelism. Since I knew nothing about TV production, God told him to work for me. He showed me everything I needed to know about producing my own TV show.

We agreed to do one show. And just as I had been surprised years earlier with radio, I discovered I was good at television too.

It got even better. We agreed to do more shows, but we were commuting to Canada once a month to produce them. This was very difficult, so God made it easy. I was told that David Cerullo, head of the Inspiration Network (INSP), had moved to a new studio in South Carolina and wanted to sell his old studio in Charlotte, NC. After a walk-through of the building, we could sense that the design was a better fit for us than for him. We paid David and purchased our current studio.

Can you see why I can't take any credit for all I am doing? God has done it all.

In 1996, I launched a weekly TV show called *It's Supernatural!*, which reaches millions around the world. The plan was simple: Each episode would share stories of supernatural healings, dreams, and visions from God, near-death experiences, and angelic encounters. We started *It's Supernatural!* to reach Jewish people. Since the Jewish people require a sign, the supernatural is key to opening their hearts to the fact that God is real and they can know Him through salvation today.

I quickly discovered that media can do more than transmit communication. It can transfer encounter.

People would write to us and say they felt God's Presence while watching a program in their living rooms. Others would tell me they were healed while watching the broadcast, like the testimonies you will read in the next chapter.

At first, this surprised me. But then I realized something: God is not limited by distance. If His Presence shows up in a meeting, it can also show up through a television screen.

Then God allowed us to purchase a permanent, state-of-the-art studio—advanced even by secular standards. I started thinking, "Since we have this wonderful production facility, we need our own network. And to have a network, I have to have shows." So I started producing shows in our studio, and in 2012, we launched our own TV network, the It's Supernatural Network (ISN). It offers over sixty exclusive programs produced in-house. These are shows you can't get anywhere else. They are produced just for ISN.

Reaching Israel and the Nations

A few years later, in 2016, I called the owner of Middle East TV (METV), a major television network that covers all of Israel and most of the Middle East, to buy some time on their network. To my surprise, the owner had just died, and his grandson had taken over. As we spoke, he said, "You know, Sid, I don't have a big burden for Israel."

I said, "Would you sell it?"

He said, "Yeah, that's what we're doing. We're going to sell the whole network."

I figured there was no way I could buy it, but I asked, "What would you charge me?"

He told me a price, and technically, I didn't have the money. But I said, "I'll buy it!" It was just that fast. I could buy it because in media we had to have big reserves. So we took our TV reserves and bought METV.

It was an opportunity I couldn't pass up. Can you imagine being able to get into every home in Israel with the gospel? I mean, it was unbelievable to me. So, long story short, I immediately jumped on a plane the next day, and I signed and purchased it. God provided exactly what we needed.

METV is part of the basic cable and satellite package for all subscribers in Israel, reaching a potential audience of half a billion people across the Middle East via satellite. Broadcasting seven days a week, twenty-four hours a day, METV has uninterrupted service.

We took the programming we had from ISN that was suitable for Israel and put it on METV, but we still needed more. We didn't have enough at that time.

So I put on westerns. Why? I liked westerns. That's why! I didn't know whether Israel would like or dislike westerns. It's not part of their history. But I couldn't think of anything else to fill the time. Most Christian TV would not work in Israel. So we put on westerns and shows proving Jesus is the Messiah.

As confirmation that it's working, an evangelist who works with New Agers in Israel recently told me about a Jewish family she has witnessed to. They won't receive any Christian literature from her, but they watch my TV show faithfully and love it. This is my primary goal for *It's Supernatural!*—to reach those who are not going to hear the good news any other way. I am always amazed when I hear about the people in foreign countries who watch our show.

Since this is *the set time* for God to favor Zion for salvation, we now have enough biblical programming to replace all westerns.

We produce so many programs that it blows my mind. These are all programs that are nowhere else but on our network. I don't think anyone can appreciate the magnitude of the miracle God did. I should not have had this network. But I'm also the first Jewish man ever to own Middle East Television, which I consider the "crown jewel" of our ministry.

And God continues to preserve METV miraculously. During the 2026 Iran conflict, the devil tried to take out our transmission in the Middle East. All our equipment and offices are located on a little island a few miles off the coast of Israel called Cyprus. As retaliation for Operation Epic Fury, Iran launched hundreds of missiles and drone strikes across neighboring countries in the region. The United Kingdom base, right next door to our office on Cyprus, was hit during these retaliatory strikes. But thankfully, God protected us, and our broadcasting to the region continued without interruption.

When I see things like that, I'm reminded of how God takes the smallest desires of our hearts and turns them into something far bigger than we ever planned. As a young person, I always wanted to be involved in Broadway, movies, and things like that. I thought it looked exciting. Years later, I thought, "I wonder if I could buy a billboard in Times Square in New York City?"

Guess what? We did! We put up a billboard, and in a short period of time, 21 million people walked by it. Do you know what it said? "I'm Jewish, and I believe in Jesus," with a picture of someone Jewish.

Then I thought, "It would be impossible, but I'd like to buy ads on the most-viewed television show in Israel"—and, I might add, the rest of the world. Do you know what the most-viewed television show in Israel is? The Super Bowl.

But we did more than that. We acquired the rights to air the Super Bowl on Middle East TV, and we offered it free of charge. And then we did something really unusual. We preempted the halftime show with my testimony. Everyone had to watch it if they wanted to see the second half of the Super Bowl—and of course, they wanted to see the second half.

Then I had another idea. And when I say I had these ideas, understand that these are God-ideas. I take zero credit. If

God tells me to do it, I jump. That's what I said in that *Daily News* article, and that's me today.

The idea? I wanted to do one-minute commercials on secular TV about why Jesus is the Messiah. We ran them on Fox News, CNBC, Newsmax, and MSNBC. Then we offered my book of Jewish testimonies, *They Thought for Themselves.*

To me, these things are amazing. But God still had more in mind. He did something new. He led us not only to have outreaches for Jewish people to come to the Lord but also to have outreaches for Muslims to come to the Lord. Thousands of Muslims have come to our outreaches, and the results are the same as we see with Jewish people.

And guess what I share at these Muslim outreaches? I don't know Islam, so I share the reality of Jesus through my testimony. And the same Presence of God that falls on the Jewish people and brings them to salvation is now falling on the Muslims as well.

They find us on the Internet too. I remember getting into a taxi in Indonesia, the largest Muslim nation in the world. The driver said, "I know you. I watch you on the Internet."

Moments like that remind me how far a message can travel today. Years ago, if you wanted to share the gospel with someone in another nation, you had to physically go there. Today, a message can cross oceans instantly. And God has used that reality to open doors that never existed before.

We also have social media—a total of 6.9 million subscribers discovering that God is real, and He operates in the supernatural. Everything we do creates the opportunity for someone to know the Lord.

I am so grateful to God for allowing me the privilege of highlighting these new things. All of it amazes me. What started with a handful of interviews on a cassette recorder turned into people all over the world hearing that the God of the Bible is still real today.

I can't take credit because I didn't plan any of this. It was all God. He showed up in my very first encounter with Him, and He has continued to show up every time He is needed and invited in my life and ministry. And as long as He shows up, I continue to say yes.

Chapter 8

FIFTY YEARS OF GOD SHOWING UP

PEOPLE HAVE ASKED me whether I still believe in Jesus as passionately as I did in the beginning. They also wonder if I could have just imagined that first encounter with His Presence.

I tell them my faith is stronger now than ever because the Spirit of God literally lives inside me. As I am writing this, I feel His Presence. It's like rivers of living water flowing through my body. It's wonderful and better than any high someone can have with drugs or alcohol.

I know Messiah Jesus as a friend, and in His name I have seen sickness leave people and more miracles than I can count. On my radio and TV shows, I have interviewed thousands of people who have had their own miraculous and amazing encounters with Him.

This has been the story of my life: When you invite Him, God shows up.

Not just once. Not occasionally. Not only in certain seasons. He showed up again and again—in different decades, on different continents, and in different circumstances.

I have seen thousands of lives transformed when people came to know Jesus for themselves. My entire Jewish family eventually came to believe in Messiah Jesus.

This is what I have discovered after walking with God for over fifty-five years. He is personal and interested in every aspect of my life. He is constantly smiling upon me and is always happy to see me. He is proud of me. Not for what I do but for who I am. I am His son! I walked for thirty years without His favor. And now I am walking in His favor. Trust me. His favor is better!

His love is very different from human love. He sent His Son to forgive me of my sins before I even knew He was real or that I was a sinner. When I had my encounter with Him, I didn't even know about asking for forgiveness of sin. I was overwhelmed by His love, and He captured my heart. Then I found that the sins I thought were important for my happiness gradually disappeared. Even stubborn sins could not remain in the Presence of His magnificent love.

This chapter is not about what I did right or how I learned along the way. It is about what God did and continues to do.

There were times I didn't know what would happen next. I didn't know how long an opportunity would last, or whether a door would stay open. But I learned that God doesn't wait for everything to make sense before He reveals Himself. He shows up right in the middle of the questions.

And in all transparency, I still operate in awe and faith today, waiting for the Greater Glory, which I know will come any second now.

Looking back over five decades, almost everything around me has changed. Audiences have changed. Culture has shifted. Technology has advanced. Even the language the church uses has changed.

But the Presence of God never changed, and it needed no introduction.

I watched people who had never been in a setting like that before recognize God without instruction. I watched Jewish people and believers from vastly different backgrounds respond to the same Presence with the same awareness.

I have seen God show up and miracles happen without me even laying my hands on people. It just erupts all over the auditorium.

It doesn't matter whether I'm in my living room Bible study with ten people or in Israel with well over one thousand unsaved Jewish Israelis, God always shows up! He always demonstrates miracles. And when that happens, almost all the unsaved are saved!

God's Presence is not limited to a culture, a generation, or a certain way of doing things. When He shows up, people know it. No one has to announce Him. His Presence speaks for itself.

This is why I have never been concerned about making God relevant. He does not need our help staying current. He is the same yesterday, today, and forever (Heb. 13:8).

Testimonies of God's Power and Presence

I thought you might enjoy a few of the many letters we receive about miracles happening through our TV show, our website, our social media, and our in-person meetings.

> I was diagnosed with scoliosis at a young age. Then Sid Roth said the Lord was healing people with back

issues, and my back went straight. I thank the Lord for healing me and for using Sid Roth to proclaim it.

—Jennifer

My mom's neck was swollen, and she was in a lot of pain and couldn't move her arm due to shoulder surgery. Two weeks later, she was watching *It's Supernatural!* on YouTube, and as you were praying, she received healing! She could then move her arm without any pain at all, and the swelling left her neck! Glory to God who worked through that prayer. God showed my mom His love and mercy.

—Anonymous

Sid was interviewing someone but stopped and said someone's neck is healed—move your neck from side to side. That was me! I have suffered from a neck injury for forty-five years! And now it's healed. Praise the Lord! Thank You, Jesus!

—Anonymous

I have never, in all my seventy years, seen or experienced a miracle. Then you told people to hold the area where they had issues, and then you prayed. I have had a terrible cough for the last week. I was even coughing during the episode. When you had those watching hold the affected area, I felt foolish, but I put my hands on my throat...and now I can breathe deeply and have no sign of that persistent cough! Praise the Lord, and thank you, Sid!

—James

I was driving to work thinking about how I needed to go to the chiropractor for my neck pain but not wanting to have to spend the money as we are on a tight budget paying for daycare for our two young sons. At work I was watching a YouTube of your show that was filmed eighteen years ago, and you said, "Someone with a neck problem is healed right now," and I felt a wave go through my neck at that very moment, and I reached up to touch my neck, and there was no more tightness anywhere and no pain when I turned my head! Praise the Lord!

—Amanda

Your ministry has been a blessing for me. I am a medical doctor by profession and was diagnosed with hepatitis B last year. I was devastated but then caught an episode of your show about healing and began confessing my healing. Then a month later, the Holy Spirit confirmed my healing in a dream. That day, I asked one of our clinical workers, who is a pastor's wife, if she was ready to put some shame on the devil, and then we prayed, and she drew my blood. The results came back negative! May God bless your ministry abundantly as you touch and transform so many lives!

—Nsakala

I had uterus cancer that spread to other organs. I read Sid's book on healing, took communion daily, and began proclaiming the healing scriptures, and within six weeks, I was completely healed!

—Letha

An atheist friend turned me on to your show because he would watch the episodes and mock them. I watched the first episode he sent to me, and I have to tell you that God got the last laugh because I've now been watching *It's Supernatural!* for almost a year and don't miss an episode. God used an atheist to bring me to Him through your show!

—Chris

I was a Hindu and had no peace, no love, no health, and no stability in my life. I was severely depressed and hopeless, and my soul was almost dead. Then God led me to your show last year. I watch *It's Supernatural!* twice a day, and I've come to know about the Real Living God, Yahweh, the Heavenly Father, Yahshua Jesus, and the Holy Spirit. Now I know the God of Abraham, Isaac, and Jacob is our Real God and Jesus is our Savior, Lord, and King. I have given my heart to Him, and now the God of Israel is my God. Amen! I speak blessings over you, your guests, and your family.

—Anonymous

I used to treat the Pentecostal Christians as those peddling a false gospel and speaking gibberish they call the gift of tongues. It was offensive to me. However, after watching your TV program *It's Supernatural!* for a while now and reading your book *They Thought for Themselves*, I've come to believe that God not only saves from sin but is still healing bodies. Thanks for opening my eyes to the miraculous.

—Charles

> I was up late one night and saw one of Sid's shows, prayed the prayer, and was set free from a ten-year cocaine addiction that had cost me millions of dollars! From that one episode, my life has made a complete U-turn! I was headed to hell, and now I am saved. Love your show! Keep up the great work for the Lord!
>
> —Anonymous

After decades of hearing testimonies like these and watching what happens when people encounter God, I've come to understand something: The supernatural isn't rare. It's how God reveals Himself.

Why Fifty Years Was Preparation, Not the Climax

It would be easy to look back over more than fifty years of God showing up and assume that I've reached my destination, that everything God intended to do has already been accomplished. But the more I reflect, the clearer something becomes. It was preparation, and we're just getting started.

For some time now, I have sensed that God was preparing His people for what is coming. I call it the Greater Glory, and I will explain it in the third part of this book.

But I can tell you this right now. It will require courage. It will require obedience. And it will require people who know God's Presence and are ready to respond.

I believe we are entering a time unlike anything we've seen before. The same God who has revealed Himself for decades is about to reveal Himself in even greater ways.

And something else is revealed at the same time. When God shows up, it reveals what's really in our hearts. It reveals whether we are prepared to move with Him.

As I think back over these years, I realize that I never once said to myself, "This is too hard. This is getting old. I'm tired. I'm weary. I need a break." That thinking was not in my DNA. The passion God put in my heart to win Jewish people to the Lord has overcome every obstacle. I have kept my eye on the prize and never looked back.

Throughout the years, *every time* I've shared my testimony, God confirmed it with supernatural fruit! My goal in this section of the book has been to share about the years of miracles since my salvation and how the events that marked my coming to the Lord were only the beginning.

I mentioned earlier that I see my own story mirrored in the way God called a man named Saul and transformed him into the apostle Paul. I don't think Paul had any idea how far God would take him. I certainly didn't! But here is what I know with absolute certainty: The same God who moved then is moving now!

As good as His Presence and miracles and salvations have been over the past fifty years, they are nothing compared with what He has in store for me at age eighty-five. I feel like the coming shift will charge my ministry to release the greatest Glory, the greatest miracles, and the most salvations in history! And if He does this for me at eighty-five, what will He do for you?

I expect many reading this book to be physically healed and filled with the Greater Glory. Get ready for the most exciting revelation of *The Glory Story* next!

PART III

THE GLORY STORY

The Mark, the Decision, and the Fulfillment of the Age

Chapter 9

WHAT ARE WE MISSING?

SEVERAL YEARS AGO, a friend of mine—the pastor of a large charismatic church—had a supernatural experience while he was visiting the Great Synagogue in Jerusalem. As he was praying, Jesus came to him and said, "I would be more at home in this building than in your church."

That statement should stop us all in our tracks.

Why would Jesus say something like that? It wasn't a criticism of Gentile believers. There are many who love God deeply and hunger for more of His Presence. But many believers do not recognize that something vital is missing. They don't recognize the importance of their biblical Jewish heritage.

When that connection is missing, something in our understanding of God's purpose is incomplete. Isaiah paints a simple but powerful picture when he says Israel is like a branch or sprout: "A shoot will come up from the stump of Jesse; from his roots a Branch will bear fruit" (Isa. 11:1). The Jewish people are the natural branches. And Gentile believers have been grafted into that same tree.

Even the language points us there. The Hebrew root is *netzer*—a shoot, a branch that grows out from a living tree.

A branch does not create its own life. It lives because it is connected to the tree. When you say, "I'm a Christian or Gentile believer," what you are actually saying is, "I have been grafted in." This is your spiritual ID. You did not start the story. God brought you into it.

Think about that. Gentile believers are not a separate tree. They are grafted into the same one. That means the church did not replace Israel. It joined Israel.

Unfortunately, over the centuries, that truth was forgotten. Instead of seeing themselves as partners in God's plan, many Christians began to view the Jewish people as outsiders. In some cases, Christians even believed that God had rejected Israel entirely and replaced them with the church.

But the Bible never teaches that.

Paul actually warns Gentile believers about this kind of thinking. He says, "Do not boast against the [natural] branches" (Rom. 11:18). Why? Because the root supports the branches—not the other way around. The Amplified Bible puts it this way: "Do not boast over the [broken] branches and exalt yourself at their expense. If you do boast and feel superior, remember that it is not you who supports the root, but the root that supports you."

Letting Go of Inherited Beliefs and Traditions

Many years ago, I heard about a unique tradition at an Orthodox synagogue in Washington, DC. Whenever someone went to the platform to read from the Torah, he would bend his knees and lower his head about a foot, and then stand back up before he got to the Torah scroll. After attending for a while, a curious member asked, "Rabbi, why do we dip so low before reading the Torah?"

The rabbi explained that the synagogue had previously been in the basement of another building. Just in front of the Torah was a low water pipe. The only way to get to the Scriptures without hitting your head was to dip low.

The pipe was gone, but the posture remained.

As a Jewish man, I have experienced enough tradition to last a lifetime.

When I encountered Jesus at the age of thirty, I expected to enter this new life free from religious traditions. I expected to find churches full of supernatural experiences—healing the sick and hearing God's voice.

But instead, I experienced one of the biggest shocks of my life. I discovered that there are very few miracles, even in believing, Spirit-filled churches. I found that many Christians say they believe in God. They think they're going to heaven. But instead of living with Jesus as Lord, many treat Him more like their servant—someone there to help them when they need it. Many Christians are inheriting religious traditions just like the Jewish people. They go through the motions and attend church when they're expected to, but they never surrender their lives and make Jesus their Lord.

I saw that many churches have become little more than human warehouses. People come in, sit, listen, and leave. They're made to feel acceptable to God without ever dealing with the issue of sin or repentance. They become spectators instead of participants in God's plan.

Surprised by what I found, I began to study the history of the early church in the Book of Acts. And when I did, something remarkable happened. The blinders of tradition fell from my eyes. I started seeing the Scriptures in a completely different light.

Now I understand why there are so few miracles in churches. Now I understand why there is so little compassion for the lost and the poor. Now I understand why the same sins that fill secular society so often fill the church as well. And now I understand how we have grieved the Holy Spirit—through ignorance, compromise, tradition, and the fear of man.

But here's the good news.

God has been waiting for a generation of believers who will follow the cloud of His Presence just as the Israelites followed the cloud in the wilderness. And I believe that cloud is moving again.

The question is: Will you follow the cloud to Glory, or will you stay where you are, comfortable in your old ways? Only a few of the older generation entered the Promised Land. The rest saw it from a distance but never stepped into it.

Just as God had a specific plan for the Israelites to enter the Promised Land, He also gave them a pattern for entering His Glory. God said to Moses, "See that you make all things according to the *pattern*" (Heb. 8:5, emphasis added). The pattern is God's bridge to intimacy. When the pattern is right, the Glory shows up.

The pattern also leads to unity between Jew and Gentile. I believe that today God is calling us to a new level in which both Jewish and Gentile believers will come together as *one new man*—yielded to His Spirit and walking in power.

"For I am about to do something new. See, I have already begun!" (Isa. 43:19, NLT).

The One New Humanity

God never intended to start a new religion. It's not Judaism and Christianity, two streams of God, but the convergence of Jew and Gentile into one stream that Paul called the "one new man." God's plan has always been to gather everything together in the Messiah (Eph. 1:10). He tells us how He will do this:

> For He Himself is our peace, who has made *both* [Jew and Gentile] *one*, and has broken down the middle wall of separation…to create in Himself *one new man*… in whom you also are being built together for a *dwelling place* of God in the Spirit.
>
> —Ephesians 2:14–15, 22, NKJV, emphasis added

Paul says that in Messiah He created "one new man" (Eph. 2:15) or "one new humanity." He was describing something brand new—a species that never existed before.

There is one body. God does not see competing identities—He sees His Son. Jesus (Yeshua) is the embodiment of the one new man Paul wrote about. And until His body walks in that reality, the story is not finished.

In the Spirit there is no difference between Jew and Gentile. We stand on equal ground before God. One is not greater than the other, and no one has a spiritual advantage.

But equality in the Spirit does not mean God erases our identities or callings. In the same way that men and women share equal standing before God while carrying different roles, Jewish and Gentile believers also have unique callings within the body of Messiah.

This did not erase cultural differences. Jewish believers remained Jewish. Gentile believers remained Gentile. But their identity in Messiah united them in a deeper way.

We need each other. When these callings come together as God intended, something explosive happens. Dead religion gives way to living Glory. Faith becomes relational again. Gratitude replaces entitlement. Humility returns. The Glory of God increases.

The Book of Acts shows us what that looks like. The early church was filled with the supernatural. People were healed. Demons were cast out. Miracles occurred regularly.

Why? Because the church was functioning the way God designed it—Jew and Gentile together. One body. One Spirit. One Messiah.

Why is this so important? Because not only has the enemy tried to destroy Jewish people century after century, but he has also worked overtime to keep both Jewish believers and Gentile believers apart. Jesus prayed in John 17 that His followers would be one, and in the first century, there were really only two groups present—Jew and Gentile. When those two become one, Jesus said the result would be that "the world will believe" (v. 21, NLT).

That is why the dividing wall between Jew and Gentile had to come down. Jesus didn't come to start a Gentile religion or to erase Israel. He came to remove the barrier between the two and create one new humanity—one body that becomes a dwelling place for God.

This unity was always God's plan. In fact, when Jews and Gentiles come together in Messiah the way God intended, something powerful is released. I believe it triggers a supernatural harvest. When the two become one new man, there will be a massive release of power to evangelize the world and bring in a great harvest of souls.

One Body, Distinct Callings

Equal standing before God does not mean identical assignments.

The Jewish people carry a calling tied to land, covenant, and destiny. Whether they recognize it or not, they are tethered to Israel by divine purpose.

But the calling does not end there. Jewish believers carry a distinct mandate that Scripture spells out plainly: The word of the Lord will go forth from Jerusalem to the nations. Scripture points to a day when instruction and revelation flow outward from Israel to the world (Isa. 2:3). That is more than symbolic—it is prophetic order. God chose Israel not only as the birthplace of Messiah but also as the launch point of revelation, both at the beginning and the end.

Gentile believers carry a calling just as specific and just as essential. Paul tells us that salvation came to the Gentiles to provoke Israel to jealousy (Rom. 11:11). That means Gentile believers are meant to live in such authentic relationship with God, such tangible encounter with the Messiah of Israel, that Jewish people recognize what has been missing.

We need each other.

When Jew and Gentile honor God's design rather than competing for position, something explosive happens. What has been dormant comes alive. What has been religious becomes powerful. The church does not shrink—it ignites with the Glory of God.

The Deeper Meaning of the Prodigal Son

Scripture shows us where the tension between the Jewish people and the Gentile church lies. Jewish people seek signs and miracles. Gentile believers seek inheritance. I compare the jealousy between Jews and Gentiles to Jesus' parable of the prodigal son. (See Luke 15:11–32.) You may have heard other applications of this parable, but this is what God has shown me.

The younger son is a type of the Jewish people. The older son is a type of the Gentile church. When the younger son returned home, the father (a type of Father God) held a great celebration with food, music, and dancing. The older brother was jealous. Luke 15:28 says that he was angry and resolved not to go to the celebration. The older brother did not understand that the father longed to be reconciled to the younger brother.

Many Gentiles do not understand the *one new man*. They do not realize that the Jewish person must be grafted into the body of Messiah to have the wedding supper of the Lamb (the heavenly feast enjoyed by Messiah and His bride, the church). The older brother cannot comprehend the truth expressed by Jesus that He would not return until the Jewish people are restored to the Father (Matt. 23:39). He cannot see that by being in the seed of Abraham, everything the Father has is already his (Luke 15:31).

After two thousand years of living out in the world, we Jewish believers have a lot of rough edges. Gentile Christians (older brothers) have a sweetness about them because of generations of knowing the Messiah. As Jewish believers, we desperately need to be embraced by our older brothers.

There is one body. The body of Messiah is not Messianic Jewish and Gentile Christian. It is not two streams having joint meetings. When God sees the body, He does not see Jew and Gentile, male and female; He sees His Son, Jesus. He is the One New Man, the King of the Jews!

The Moment Everything Changes

Romans 11:11 tells us something the church can no longer afford to ignore: God chose Gentile believers as the very means to draw the Jewish people back to Himself. It's not an option. It's an assignment.

Provoking Israel to jealousy does not mean arguing theology. It means living with something so real, so supernatural, and so filled with the Presence of God that Jewish people say, "What do you have that we don't?" It means walking in peace that can't be shaken, families that are healed, love that endures pressure, and power that comes only from intimacy with God.

The enemy knows what is at stake just as clearly as God does. If he can keep precious Jewish souls from being restored to God, then he can prevent the full manifestation of God's Glory on the body of Messiah. So he works hard to deceive the church into thinking Jewish evangelism is unnecessary, offensive, or already taken care of by God through some other means.

Instead of provoking jealousy, much of the church has done the opposite. We have pushed Jewish people away—sometimes through silence, sometimes through fear, and sometimes through a version of Christianity stripped of God's power and Presence.

Some of that silence has been deliberate, shaped by specific teachings that have spread widely. Many Christians have accepted the idea that Jewish people are under judgment and that God has blinded their eyes to the gospel, so there is no point in witnessing to them. Others believe God has a separate plan for Jewish people to be saved without Jesus. And some believe Jewish people will only come to salvation after the rapture, during the tribulation, so the church's role now is simply to wait.

These are not minor theological disagreements. They are doctrines of demons meant to plunder heaven and populate hell!

Much of this traces back to a misreading of Romans 11:25, which says "a partial hardening has come upon Israel until the fullness of the Gentiles has come in." The word translated "fullness" is better rendered "maturity." Paul is not describing a fixed quota of Gentile souls after which Jewish hearts automatically open. He is describing a condition—the maturity of the Gentile church.

It is not kind or culturally sensitive to avoid sharing the gospel with Jewish people. Many Christians are taking a "do not evangelize" approach for the sake of unity with the Jewish people. Only if a Jewish person asks them about salvation will they share the good news—and sometimes not even then!

This is the opposite of what Paul preached. Referring specifically to the Jewish people, Paul said, "How then shall they call on Him in whom they have not believed? And how shall they believe in Him of whom they have not heard?" (Rom. 10:14). "Faith comes by hearing, and hearing by the word of God" (Rom. 10:17). Paul never once said to withhold the good news from the Jewish people. If a Gentile Christian had not shared the gospel with me, my entire Jewish family and I would have died without knowing the Messiah.

When the church is mature—when Gentile believers are walking in the power of the Holy Spirit—there will be a Jewish revival unlike anything the world has ever seen. Only the anointing of the Holy Spirit can break the yokes of unbelief that have held Jewish hearts for millennia. That breakthrough happens after Jewish hearts are opened by supernatural love that carries peace, healing, and authority through God's Presence.

Every great move of God comes down to individuals who are willing to take responsibility for what they see. Not what they were taught. Not what they were told. But what God Himself has made plain in His Word.

That is where the story turns next.

Chapter 10

THEY THOUGHT FOR THEMSELVES

Years ago, God instructed me in a dream to write a book of Jewish testimonies. He told me that more Jewish people would come to know Him through that book than through anything I had done up to that point. I titled it *They Thought for Themselves.* This book was a collection of testimonies from Jewish men and women who chose to follow Yeshua despite tradition, pressure, and cost—people who encountered truth and took responsibility for what they had seen.

At the time, I understood that title as uniquely Jewish. What I did not yet realize was that the same demand—to think for oneself in the Presence of God—would one day confront the church.

People who think for themselves refuse to let tradition or fear decide truth for them when God has made Himself known. They do not trade conviction for consensus, nor do they confuse silence with wisdom. And history shows us something sobering: When pressure increases, the majority is often sincere but often wrong.

People who think for themselves change the world.

When Truth Demands Responsibility

For Jewish people, recognizing Messiah has never been a matter of convenience. It has always required courage—the courage to think for oneself. At some point, every Jewish person who encounters Yeshua must answer a question no one else can answer for them: Is this true?

That question risks family, community, and identity, which is why, for generations, many have chosen safety over certainty—deferring decisions rather than confronting them.

I understand that tension. But I can honestly say that when I encountered God, any hesitation I might have had vanished. I knew something real had happened to me, and I knew others needed to experience it too. Wherever I went, I spoke. Whoever stood in front of me heard my testimony. I didn't worry about the outcome. I had tasted something undeniable, and silence was no longer an option.

That's what happens when truth becomes real. History shows this again and again—not only among Jewish believers but among Christians as well. Everyone who truly recognizes what God is doing eventually faces the same decision: Stay quiet or step forward.

One such believer was Dietrich Bonhoeffer.

Christian Courage During the Holocaust

Bonhoeffer lived in Nazi Germany, a time when anti-Semitism had been normalized, justified, and even defended theologically. German Christians still read Scripture, still sang hymns, still taught doctrine. But the majority postponed obedience in the name of caution. Bonhoeffer recognized what many refused to see: When hatred toward the Jewish people is tolerated and silence is framed as wisdom, the church has already drifted from God's heart.

Bonhoeffer understood that staying silent in the face of injustice isn't neutral. It means you're participating. He thought for himself in the Presence of God—and paid for it with his life. History honors him now, but in real time, his obedience was lonely, costly, and misunderstood. That is almost always how it is.

But Bonhoeffer was not the only one who made that choice. In southern France, an entire Christian village followed the leadership of André Trocmé, a pastor who openly preached that Christians must protect Jewish people because Jesus Himself was Jewish. They established what would come to be known as the Kitchen Resistance movement against the Nazis.[1]

The village hid about five thousand Jewish people—most of them children—during World War II, saving them from Nazi concentration camps. What's more, they cared for these refugee children in their own homes and educated them in their own schools for the rest of the war. Trocmé taught his congregation that obedience to God outweighed obedience to the state—and that faith without action was hollow.

They were interrogated, threatened, and watched. Yet they remained obedient.

No one knew their story until years later. That is often how it is with those who think for themselves.

I cannot share examples from the Holocaust without mentioning Corrie ten Boom and her family. They were not activists. They were believers who took the Bible seriously. When the Gestapo hunted Jewish people, Corrie's family hid them in their home. They were betrayed, arrested, and sent to concentration camps. Corrie survived. Her father and sister Betsie did not.

Corrie never considered herself heroic. She believed obedience was simply required. And after the war—when many Christians chose silence out of guilt or fear—she continued to affirm God's covenant with Israel and the necessity of Messiah.

Moral Clarity in the Modern Age

It might surprise you to learn that throughout his life, Dr. Martin Luther King Jr. was a strong supporter of Israel and Jewish people. Many people today don't realize that. But whenever he heard someone denounce Israel, he spoke up. He stood firmly for the Jewish people and for the Zionist cause.

Just two weeks before he was assassinated in 1968, Dr. King spoke these words to the Rabbinical Assembly:

> Peace for Israel means security, and we must stand with all our might to protect its right to exist....I see Israel as one of the great outposts of democracy in the world, and a marvelous example of what can be done, how desert land can be transformed into an oasis of brotherhood and democracy. Peace for Israel means security, and that security must be a reality.[2]

Dr. King also believed that histories of shared struggles connected the Black and Jewish communities and that we needed to stand up for one another's rights.

Dr. King's march on Selma is famous. But did you know that Rabbi Abraham Joshua Heschel walked right by his side? The two men became close friends and remained so until King's death.

In fact, just ten days before he was assassinated, King spoke at a celebration honoring Rabbi Heschel that was attended by more than one thousand rabbis. And when Heschel later spoke at Dr. King's funeral, he said, "Martin Luther King is a voice, a vision, and a way. I call upon every Jew to harken to his voice, to share his vision, to follow in his way."[3]

King refused to follow the crowd. He spoke truth about prejudice when it would have been easier to stay silent. And his words remind us of something important: Every generation must decide whether it will repeat the errors of the past or stand for what is right.

I saw this same kind of courage in Derek Prince. He was a brilliant Bible teacher, educated at Cambridge, but what impressed me most was his commitment to Scripture.

Like Bonhoeffer and Corrie ten Boom in their generation, Derek refused to simply accept the prevailing thinking of the church. If tradition didn't line up with the Bible, Derek went with the Bible.

At a time when many Christians had forgotten the Jewish roots of their faith, he quietly but firmly reminded believers that God's covenant with the Jewish people had never been canceled. He once wrote,

> Almost limitless misunderstanding, ignorance, and distortion have pervaded the church for many centuries concerning the identity of Israel. This seems extraordinary to me because the statements in the Bible regarding Israel are so clear. Nevertheless, the minds of multitudes of Christians seem to be clouded in regard to the application of the name of Israel.[4]

Derek also said that a Christian who has no particular love for the Jewish people and Israel is "deficient" and "incomplete."[5] He encouraged Christians to read the Scriptures for themselves and to take God at His Word when it came to Israel.

Derek thought for himself—because he wanted to be faithful to the Word of God. And because he did, many believers rediscovered God's heart for the Jewish people.

Sadly, the hostility Derek warned about has not disappeared. In fact, anti-Semitism continues to rise; there is no shortage of opportunities for the church to stand with the Jewish people.

In recent years, we've seen attacks on synagogues in places like Pittsburgh; Poway, California; Colleyville, Texas; West Bloomfield, Michigan; and most recently, London. The hatred directed toward the Jewish people has not disappeared. But moments like these also present the church with a choice: Will believers remain silent, or will we stand with the Jewish people when it matters most?

The time has come to think for ourselves.

Each of us has to answer some very personal questions. Will we follow what Scripture says, even when it challenges what we've always believed? Will we honor Israel the way God does, even when the rest of the world is standing against them? Will we follow the leading of the Holy Spirit when He asks us to step outside what feels safe?

Each of us must decide whether we will follow what God says or let societal pressure decide for us.

In the days ahead, it will not be enough just to recognize what God is doing. We will have to know how to flow in obedience to Him. He is looking for people who will say yes and move with Him. And the only way to learn how to move with God is to encounter Him when He shows up.

THINKING FOR OURSELVES IN THE FINAL HOUR

As we move closer to the end of the age, the pressure is going to increase—not only from the world but from inside the church itself. Believers will have to learn to think for themselves. They will have to test what they hear and measure everything against the Word of God.

If any message contradicts Scripture, it is not from God. In the final hour, thinking for yourself will not mean standing alone. It will mean standing with God's heart—even when it costs you something.

This is preparation for the Greater Glory.

History shows us that God always prepares a people before He pours out power. Bonhoeffer prepared through obedience before clarity was popular. The Ten Booms prepared through action when compassion demanded risk.

Others have stood in their hour. Now the church is being asked to stand in ours—before the Glory intensifies, before pressure peaks, before silence hardens into resistance. It reminds me of the classic tale by Hans Christian Andersen, *The Emperor's New Clothes.*

In the story a proud ruler becomes obsessed with wearing garments that will display his greatness. Two swindlers arrive in his kingdom, claiming they can weave a magnificent fabric invisible to anyone who is foolish or unfit for office. Not wanting to appear incompetent, the emperor's advisers pretend they can see the cloth. The emperor does the same. Soon the entire court joins the charade, each person afraid to admit the truth. At last, the emperor parades through the city wearing nothing at all—until a child, unafraid of ridicule or consequence, blurts out what everyone else knows but will not say: "He isn't wearing anything!"

And what's the moral of that story? We must think for ourselves. In fact, it will be essential that we do so in the days ahead as the Glory of God's Presence increases.

Chapter 11

THE GREATER GLORY

WE ARE LIVING in a moment that history has not yet given a name—but it will.

Some seasons are recognized only after you have passed through them. While you are in them, you may not fully realize what God is doing. But later, you look back and see that everything changed.

I believe we are living in one of those moments right now.

I believe we are about to see the greatest move of God the world has ever seen—and that it may happen sooner than most people realize.

A MOMENT BETWEEN MOVES

In my opinion, for the last ten years, we have been living between two moves of God.

That space—when old things begin to fade and the next thing has not yet fully appeared—can feel uncertain. But over the years, I have learned something about the way God moves. Before God releases something new, He often asks His people to release what they have become comfortable with.

God doesn't lead us forward while we're holding on to yesterday. If letting go of the past makes you anxious, ask God to show you what He is preparing. I promise it is something far greater than anything you or I have experienced before.

The Angel of Change

Pastor Darren Canning once visited our studio as a guest on *It's Supernatural!* and gave me one of his prophetic paintings. He titled it *The Angel of Change.* Darren told me he painted it after coming to our studio and seeing this angel there.

Today, that painting hangs in my office, and every time I look at it, I am reminded that God is always moving.

Over the past couple of years, we have experienced many changes, and those changes have only reinforced something deep in my spirit: God is still in control.

That painting reminds me not to resist what God is doing but to embrace it—to remain expectant for His next move and never fear the change that comes when God begins to reposition His people. Because, throughout history, whenever God is about to release something greater, change almost always comes first.

God moved at creation. He moved at Pentecost. He has moved in every generation that made room for Him. And whenever God moves, everything changes.

But this coming move will require something from us. We must learn to listen more carefully for the voice of the Lord. We must move in His timing rather than trying to force things according to our own timetable.

I believe God is already beginning to move in ways that are about to surpass anything we have seen before.

And I believe the change we are moving toward is what the Bible calls the Greater Glory.

The Greater Glory

The Greater Glory is a term I have used for years. It comes straight out of the Bible.

The Word of God says the whole earth will be filled with the Glory of the Lord in the last days. Something new is coming.

Isaiah 43:18–21 says:

> Do not remember the former things, nor consider the things of old. See, I will do a new thing, now it shall spring forth; shall you not be aware of it? I will even make a way in the wilderness, and rivers in the desert… to give drink to My people, My chosen ones. This people I have formed for Myself; they shall declare My praise.

I believe we are standing at the edge of the greatest outpouring of God's Glory in history. Scripture speaks of a latter Glory that will be greater than the former (Hag. 2:9). As His Glory increases, everything hidden is exposed. That is why the present moment feels so intense. Haggai 2:9 says, "'The glory of this latter temple shall be greater than the former,' says the Lord of hosts."

I have proclaimed this message for decades, even when few were listening. At times, I have felt like John the Baptist. But even when the rest of the world seemed to forget, I never stopped proclaiming it.

God gave me a glimpse of what this coming Greater Glory looks like, and it has never left me. People sometimes ask me how the Lord revealed the coming Greater Glory to me. The answer is simple. I have a friend named Keith Ellis, a retired pastor of a church where great miracles broke out. I speak with him almost daily. As I sensed what God was about to do, we started talking about the Greater Glory in those daily conversations. Those discussions sharpened and refined my understanding of what is coming.

And I am convinced of three things: (1) It will happen any second now; (2) it will exceed anything we have imagined; and (3) it will mark God's people with clarity, authority, and peace in a time of great shaking.

Why Glory Is God's Provision for This Hour

Know this: God is not dangling the Greater Glory in front of us like a reward. He is releasing it because we will need it. Anyone who is paying attention can see it. Darkness is increasing in the world. But God's answer is not fear. His answer has always been His Presence. And in this hour, He is releasing a greater measure of His Glory.

Glory is one of the most misunderstood words in the church. Often, when people hear the word *glory*, they think of emotion, music, or moments of heightened spiritual experience. God certainly moves in those ways, but that is not what Scripture means when it speaks of the Glory of the Lord filling the earth (Hab. 2:14).

In biblical terms, *glory*—translated from the Hebrew word *Kavod*—has several meanings. It means weight or substance. God's Presence is described as weighty and tangible, filling spaces like the tabernacle. It also means splendor or majesty, conveying brilliance and the impressive Presence of God. In the temple, Glory revealed God's holiness.

Glory is God revealing Himself in a way that changes everything around Him. It separates light from darkness. It brings order where there was chaos. It establishes peace where fear once ruled.

Unlike anointing, which flows through people, Glory is God showing up Himself.

Over the years, I have watched God confirm this again and again. In seasons of anointing, people minister *with* God. In seasons of Glory, God ministers *despite* people.

This is why the final outpouring Scripture points us toward will not look like past moves. It will surpass them.

Many of the early pioneers of the Pentecostal movement understood this. Men like Smith Wigglesworth spoke not only of supernatural power but of an ever-increasing work of the Spirit. Wigglesworth once said that if the Spirit did not move, he would "move the Spirit" in faith. What he meant was that God's activity would not be limited to history. It would increase over time.

Others have described gatherings where the manifest Presence of God was so strong that miracles happened without anyone touching a person. Conviction fell without anyone arguing. Even the dead were raised.

These were glimpses of Glory. And I believe we are about to see much more. I believe the day is coming when everyone in a meeting will be healed instantly, and all the unsaved will turn to Jesus. Missing limbs and organs will be restored. Every word of prophecy will come to pass. Your energy, strength, and health at age one hundred will be as it was at thirty.

The coming outpouring will not be limited to the Gentile church. I'm convinced that Israel will experience an awakening unlike anything seen since the first century.

I have already seen the firstfruits of this. When Glory manifests, healings happen without anyone orchestrating them. People suddenly realize the pain is gone. Bodies respond. And when that happens, the gospel no longer needs to be defended. It stands on its own.

That is why love alone, while essential, is not enough. Love prepares the ground. Glory brings the harvest. Together, they look like the Book of Acts.

And when this Glory comes in its fullness, no person will receive the credit. That will be one of its defining features. It will not be about man. It will be about everyone operating in the tangible, supernatural Presence of God.

When the Greater Glory comes, no one will have to tell you God is there. Everyone will know.

Glory in Scripture

I often tell people that if you really want to understand Glory, you must go back to the very beginning—Genesis chapter 1. Darkness covered the deep, chaos was everywhere, and yet the Spirit of God was hovering over the waters. Before God spoke a single word, His Spirit was already moving. Glory was present before order appeared. God did not wait for the darkness to lift. He moved first. And that same Spirit is still hovering today, waiting for people who will recognize that Glory moves *ahead of circumstances*, not behind them.

Then God speaks: "Let there be light" (Gen. 1:3). God saw that the light was good, and He separated the light from the darkness. That light was the Glory, and that separation is one of the primary functions of Glory. When God's light increases, what was hidden becomes visible and what could be tolerated in dimness becomes impossible to ignore.

Glory is also protection and power. When the tabernacle was completed, Moses could not enter because the Glory of the Lord filled it so fully. The man who spoke with God face-to-face could not step into the fullness of His manifest Presence (Exod. 40:34–35). Later, when Solomon dedicated the temple, the priests could not stand to minister because the Glory filled the house of God. When God reveals Himself at that level, it won't be business as usual.

Glory also provides direction. There is a reason Israel followed the cloud in the wilderness. When the cloud moved, they moved. When it rested, they rested. In a season when there will be many voices, we will need direction that comes from God's Presence, not opinion.

And God's Glory establishes spiritual authority that does not need to announce itself. In Acts 5:1–11, Ananias and Sapphira fell dead because God's Presence enforced holiness. This caused a holy fear to come upon the church, and many believers were added to the kingdom.

Glory Reveals the Nature of God

Now let me take you deeper into something Moses understood. Moses once asked God, "Show me Your glory" (Exod. 33:18). That was not a request for spectacle. It was a request for revelation. The deepest question a human being can ask is: "Let me see who You really are."

I ask God almost every night and every morning to show me His Glory. And when Moses said that, God's response was one of the most important definitions of Glory in the entire Bible. God told Moses He would cause His goodness to pass before him. Glory and goodness are inseparable. Glory is not intimidation. It is not God trying to frighten people into obedience. It is God's goodness, and it's manifested by the love of God that pours out of and surrounds God Himself.

That is why Scripture repeatedly associates God's Presence with *shalom*—peace the world cannot give and cannot take away. This peace is not the absence of trouble; it is the Presence of God in the middle of trouble. It is the ability to stand steady when circumstances demand panic, the assurance that nothing can come near you unless God allows it.

When the Greater Glory comes, God is going to give us peace that the world cannot take away from us. Sickness can't take it away. Death can't take it away. I believe we are coming into a time when this peace will become so substantial that fear will lose its power over believers who live under Glory. I'm not talking about denial. I'm talking about a spiritual environment so saturated with God's Presence that it makes anxiety impossible to sustain—not because you have perfect discipline but because God's Presence is ruling your inner world.

You Were Created to Perceive the Glory of God

God created human beings with senses, and He did not abandon those senses in the spiritual realm. You were created to perceive God, not just to believe in Him. Just as you see, hear, smell, taste, and feel in the natural world, there are spiritual parallels that the Glory of God awakens.

God's Glory can be seen. Throughout Scripture, people saw His Glory. Stephen gazed into heaven and saw the Glory of God (Acts 7:55). Throughout history, artists even tried to capture what they observed on the lives of saints by painting halos above their heads. They were attempting to express a Presence—a light that could not be explained naturally. When God's Presence rests on someone, your spirit recognizes it.

God's Glory can be heard. On the day of Pentecost, the Holy Spirit came with the sound of a rushing mighty wind. Heaven is not silent, and the Presence of God is not always gentle in the way people expect. Sometimes God shakes what must be shaken so that what cannot be shaken will remain.

God's Glory can be felt. If you have ever experienced the peace of God, you know it is tangible. God's peace settles on you, steadies your heart, and aligns you with His Presence. I have watched people walk into meetings burdened and anxious and walk out completely different—because something real rested on them that had nothing to do with psychology and everything to do with the Presence of God.

God's Glory can even be smelled and tasted. At times, I have sensed fragrance in the Spirit—pure and unmistakable. I have also tasted sweetness like honey in God's Presence. God gives us these signs not to mystify us but to awaken us. God does not want us relating to Him from a distance. He wants us to recognize His nearness.

How to Sharpen Your Spiritual Senses

One of the primary ways God awakens spiritual sensitivity is through praying in tongues. In the New Testament, people spoke in languages they were never taught. This was not emotional overflow. It was supernatural access. Praying in tongues fine-tunes the spirit. It sharpens sensitivity. It multiplies effectiveness. I often say I feel incomplete—almost undressed—if I do not pray in tongues daily.

Now, I understand why some believers approach spiritual experience with caution. History has seen moments where genuine encounters with God were followed by excess, imbalance, or confusion. But Scripture doesn't deal with misuse by backing away from the truth. It deals with it by restoring God's order. God is not the author of confusion, and the Glory of God never replaces wisdom—it makes it clearer. True Glory deepens humility. It pulls you toward obedience.

If an experience pulls people away from Scripture, it isn't the Glory. If it produces pride, it isn't the Glory. And if it points to a person instead of Jesus, it certainly isn't the Glory. The most anointed person in the room isn't the loudest one. It's the one surrendered to God.

From Dwelling Among Us to Dwelling Within Us

This brings us to something very important. Glory is not only something that comes *upon* us. Glory also lives *within* us. When Jesus comes to live inside a believer, He doesn't visit. He abides. When the Holy Spirit fills us, He is not hovering nearby. He lives inside us. The Bible calls this "[Messiah] in you, the hope of glory" (Col. 1:27).

That is not just a beautiful phrase. It is the foundation of the gospel. The same Spirit who raised Jesus from the dead now lives inside every believer. And that Spirit carries the Glory of God. When you understand this, it changes how you see everything.

The Greater Glory we are talking about is not dependent on a location, a building, or a particular kind of meeting. We are not waiting for God to show up somewhere out there. We are learning how to yield to the One who already lives within us. The tabernacle pointed to this. The temple prepared the way for it. But God's plan was always people.

Then something extraordinary happened in the New Testament. In the Old Testament, the Glory of God lived in a place. In the Gospels, the Glory of God lived in a person—Jesus. But after Pentecost, the Glory of God lived in people.

Pentecost revealed the shift. Fire no longer fell on an altar. It rested on people's heads. The Glory of God was no longer confined to a building. It inhabited lives.

And this is where the Greater Glory becomes possible. In the past, the Glory of God was concentrated. Now it is multiplied. That is why the coming Greater Glory will not be carried by a few special leaders. It will be carried by a people.

The Glory must first live *within us* before it can rest *upon us* in power. External manifestations can impress crowds, but they cannot sustain a move of God. Only transformed lives can do that. When the Glory lives inside a believer, it produces stability under pressure, clarity in confusion, and authority that does not need to announce itself.

The Greater Glory cannot be carried by performance. It is carried by surrendered people.

Practical Ways to Abide in the Glory

Over the years, I've learned that while Glory cannot be controlled, there are simple, repeatable ways we can invite God's Presence into our daily lives.

Live in instant repentance. Do not allow sin to accumulate. Repent the moment conviction comes, while the heart is still soft. Delay dulls sensitivity. The operative word is *instant*!

Pray the prayer of Moses in Exodus 33:18: "Show me Your glory." This prayer invites God's manifest Presence rather than mere blessing.

Pray in tongues continually. Praying in tongues fine-tunes the spirit, sharpens sensitivity, and keeps the believer spiritually aligned and receptive.

Cultivate gratitude and thankfulness. Thanksgiving shifts awareness from circumstances to God's Presence and creates an atmosphere where Glory rests.

Speak openly about the goodness of God. Testifying to what God has done reinforces faith, releases expectation, and magnifies His Presence.

Stay consciously connected to the Holy Spirit. Glory is sustained through awareness, not effort. Remaining "plugged in" requires daily attentiveness to the Spirit's leading.

Walk in the fear of the Lord. Reverence preserves Glory. Casual religion repels it. Honor attracts it.

The Promise of the Greater Glory

As a new Jewish believer in Messiah Jesus over fifty years ago, I did not remember ever reading about the Greater Glory in the Bible. In fact, when I first searched for the phrase, only one verse appeared—this one: "The glory of this latter house will be greater than the former" (Hag. 2:9). Haggai spoke to people rebuilding after loss. They remembered former Glory and felt discouraged by comparison. God did not rebuke them for remembering the past; He corrected their expectation for the future. He told them that what was coming would be greater.

That statement is staggering if you understand what the former Glory looked like. The former Glory filled the tabernacle so powerfully that Moses could not enter. The former Glory filled the temple so completely that priests could not stand to minister. That was real Glory. And God says the latter Glory will surpass it.

That realization forced a question I could not ignore. Where was the divine Presence in the former house? Scripture is clear: It was in the temple—specifically, in the holy of holies. So where is the Greater Glory we are promised—the Glory that will bring greater peace?

The new house or temple is our physical body. God says the holy of holies is located in our hearts.

> On the last and greatest day of the feast, Jesus stood and cried out, "If anyone is thirsty, let him come to Me and drink. He who believes in Me, as the Scripture has said, out of his heart shall flow rivers of living water."
>
> —John 7:37–38

How much of God's Glory will flow out of a believer? A few drops? No, rivers!

How is that possible? The Greater Glory will allow demonic barriers to the full biblical supernatural to be lifted. Then we will truly live as Jesus described in John 14:12: "He who believes in Me will do the works that I do also. And he will do greater works than these." Consider what He is saying. The dead were raised. Limbs were restored. Tumors disappeared. Diseases vanished. And Jesus says greater is coming.

The difference is not the source; it is the distribution. The new house, the new temple, is not a building. It is our bodies as believers. What was once confined to the holy of holies is now carried within God's people. In the Gospels, Glory was concentrated in one person, Yeshua—walking among the people. In Acts, Glory was multiplied through a people filled with the Spirit.

This is why I believe we are about to see massive creative miracles—miracles that do not fit old categories. You are going to witness massive evangelism that does not rely on persuasion, debate, or pressure but on Presence. People will recognize what arguments could never convince because God's goodness will become undeniable. It will be unlike anything any generation on earth has ever seen.

Before the full Glory comes, I can tell you how you're going to recognize it. There will be a restored emphasis on the fear of the Lord—not a fearful spirit but a holy reverence, the kind we see in Acts chapter 9. This is not living in fear but living with an awareness that says, "I don't want to displease You, God." Do you see the difference?

Without the fear of the Lord, the Glory has no place to rest. But when the Glory comes, something shifts. Casual Christianity doesn't sit right anymore. Indifference starts to fall off. You become aware of God in a way that changes how you live.

There's a substance to His Presence that is very real. It brings a kind of joy that isn't shallow and a freedom that doesn't lead you into compromise.

This is why the fear of the Lord matters. Without it, discernment weakens and confusion increases. But when the fear of the Lord is present, clarity comes.

The days ahead will require more than faith. They will require clear sight. God is not releasing a greater measure of His Glory so His people can feel impressive. He is releasing it because we will need His light, His protection, and His direction in an hour when darkness is increasing.

This is God's mercy. It is His provision for a people who must stand in darkness without becoming afraid, compromised, or confused.

If you think the Greater Glory is something you attend, something you watch, or something you visit when your schedule allows, you will miss what God is actually offering. Glory is not an event. It is an environment. And in the days ahead, that environment is what God's people will need.

Some believers are hungry for power but not hungry for holiness. Others want peace but resist surrender. Many say they want the Presence of God—as long as it doesn't confront what they've kept hidden.

But when God increases His Presence, everything changes. His light exposes deception. It purifies motives. It teaches us how to walk in truth.

The question is not whether the Glory is coming. The question is whether we will become the kind of people who can carry it.

This is an invitation to ask God what Moses asked Him: "Show me Your Glory."

And then make room in your life for the answer. Because God is looking for people who will become a dwelling place for His Presence.

If you have never made Jesus your Lord and Savior, now is the time. Repeat this prayer out loud:

> *Dear God, I have made mistakes, and I am sorry. I believe the blood of Jesus has washed me clean. Jesus, come and live inside me. I make You my Lord. Thank You for saving me. Amen.*

And if you are already a believer, I want to pray for you.

Father, thank You that we are Your children. Thank You that You never leave us. Fill us with Your Holy Spirit. Let us experience Your Presence in a real and transforming way so that we truly know You and walk in everything You have prepared for us. Amen.

This chapter is not meant to scare you. It is meant to prepare you.

The Greater Glory is God's answer for the hour we are living in. When His Glory increases, the church becomes what she was always meant to be—a dwelling place for God, a people marked by His Presence, and a witness who carries heaven into the earth.

But the Glory of God is never released without purpose. In the Book of Acts, when the Presence of God increased, people were saved. And the harvest that is coming will not look like anything we have seen before.

The Greater Glory is coming so that the greatest harvest in history can take place. And that harvest is inseparably connected to the Jewish people. A church that ignores Israel has missed a central part of God's end-time plan. Scripture shows us where this story is headed.

God's Glory will increase. The harvest will begin. And His covenant promises to Israel will be fulfilled. The awakening of the Jewish people will not be the end of the story. It will be the catalyst for the salvation of the world.

Everything God has spoken will come to pass. And everything I have shared in this chapter leads to the most important thing God has shown me.

Chapter 12

THE ESTHER MOMENT

CERTAIN MOMENTS IN Scripture are more than history. They are prophetic pictures that show us how God moves when the world reaches a moment of decision.

Purim is one of those moments.

Purim is a Jewish celebration that marks the day a death sentence against the Jewish people was overturned by the hand of God. It's recorded in the Book of Esther, which is often read on Purim in remembrance of what God has done.

In Esther's day, anti-Semitism reached a terrifying peak. An official decree had been signed. The destruction of the Jewish people looked like a done deal.

But what looked final in the natural was not final in the supernatural. Man's decree was not heaven's decree. What the enemy meant for annihilation, God turned into preservation. And what had been written as a death sentence became a testimony of miraculous deliverance.

When I look at what is happening in the world today, I see the same pattern unfolding. Anti-Semitism is rising. Hostility toward Israel is growing louder. The prophet Zechariah said that in the end times, all nations would turn against Israel.

But just as in Esther's day, God is not wringing His hands. God is positioning help for His people. God is awakening boldness in modern-day Mordecais and Esthers. God is overturning evil decrees.

The same God who preserved the Jewish people then is preserving them now. And *you* are part of that story because the greatest answer to anti-Semitism is not silence—it is salvation!

There has been such an increase of anti-Semitism around the world, yet at the same time, God is moving behind the scenes in ways that look very much like the Book of Esther. When I look at what's happening today, I sometimes say we are living in "Purim 2.0."

God is so brilliant that it's hard for me to keep up with Him.

THE END-TIME BOOK

For many years, I taught on the Book of Esther every year around Purim. I taught it with expectancy. And I can tell you without exaggeration that I saw more miracles when I taught on Esther than with any other message I've ever given, except my testimony of salvation.

That's when the Holy Spirit showed me something surprising. I believe the Book of Esther is *the* end-time book for the church.

Most people miss this because they read the Book of Esther as a story about bravery and favor—and those things are there—but they are not the point.

The real point is recognition. We are supposed to see ourselves in the story. Esther represents the end-time church.

When we look through this lens, we see our position, our responsibility, and our moment of decision.

The Least Likely Queen

God introduces Esther as an orphan—someone without protection, without inheritance, and without obvious authority.

She was the least likely person to become queen. Why? She had no pedigree, no royal bloodline, no social standing. And to make matters worse, there was already a chosen queen.

A miracle had to happen for Esther to become queen. First, the existing queen had to be removed. Then there was a massive beauty contest across the empire. Esther—an orphaned Jewish girl—became queen of the land.

Does that sound familiar? It does to me. That's the story of the Gentile church. A Gentile was the least likely to become royalty in God's covenant. Yet through Jesus, we are grafted into the spiritual seed of Abraham, Isaac, and Jacob. We are adopted into the family of God and brought into royalty.

And the pattern doesn't end there. Esther hid her Jewish identity until a set time in history. Likewise, the church has hidden her Jewish roots until a set time in history. And I believe—without hesitation—that set time is now.

Gentile believers, you may not realize this, but just like Esther, you are beautiful. Not just beautiful—the most beautiful in the land in God's sight. And you were chosen. He would have died just for you.

But being chosen doesn't mean being excused. That kind of favor and position always carries an assignment. Esther was not placed in the palace for personal security. She was placed there for intercession. Her position was not a reward but a responsibility. And that responsibility would eventually demand exposure.

Like Esther, the Gentile church carries a calling.

We have been granted access to Scripture, to revelation, to the Presence of God, and to global reach. Esther reminds us that being favored does not mean being shielded from consequence.

This is why the book does not soften the moment of decision. Mordecai does not reassure Esther. He does not promise safety. He does not say God will protect her no matter what she chooses. Instead, he says, "If you remain silent, deliverance will arise elsewhere—but you will not escape the cost of silence."

God's purposes will move forward with or without individual participation. The question Esther poses is not whether God will act but whether His people will be faithful when the moment requires it.

As God's Presence increases, where people stand will become very clear. Influence will be exposed for what it really is. Silence will no longer be neutral. And the church will face the same decision Esther faced. Will we stay comfortable and protected where we are, or will we step forward and obey God?

I get many letters asking why there is no mention of God's name in the Book of Esther. His name may not appear, but as Esther's story unfolds, His involvement is visible. His fingerprints are everywhere. Esther shows us how God works behind the scenes, putting people in place before the threat is announced. Her story makes clear that what looked accidental was intentional.

God had prepared everything for a sudden, supernatural turning point.

Prepared Before Action

Scripture tells us that Esther underwent twelve months of preparation before she was brought before the king—six months soaked in oil of myrrh and six months in perfumes and spices.

Esther was not being decorated; she was being changed. She was being saturated. Preparation in God is immersive. It seeps in slowly. It reshapes identity, posture, and perception. By the time Esther entered the king's presence, she carried something that could not be manufactured.

Myrrh is bitter on the outside but sweet on the inside. It speaks of suffering that produces fragrance. I often say, "Do you know what she smelled like? Heaven." That is not an exaggeration.

Scripture emphasizes aroma because aroma lingers. It fills space. It announces presence before words are spoken. Esther did not persuade the king with argument. She did not manipulate him with strategy. She carried favor that came from preparation.

This preparation of soaking in oil has a parallel for us today. Do you realize what happens when you worship God? You are soaking in the oil of the Holy Spirit. And the more you soak, the more beautiful you become in God's eyes. The more favored you become. The more Glory rests upon you.

In Matthew 25, Jesus tells a parable about ten virgins—five wise and five foolish. What was the difference? Oil. The foolish wanted the oil of the wise, but it doesn't work that way. You can't borrow intimacy. You must get your own oil by soaking in the Presence of the living God.

When you've spent time soaking in His Presence, you have the Glory of God on you. You have the King's attention. Do you understand that? You have divine favor. And like Esther, you may not realize it, but I'm telling you plainly: You are the only one who can go to the King on behalf of the Jewish people in this hour.

TRUSTING GOD FOR THE OUTCOME

Haman—who we might say represents the devil or even the spirit behind nations like ancient Persia and modern Iran—wanted to destroy every Jewish man, woman, and child. Logically, you might think he would only want to destroy those who opposed him. But the devil is not logical. Just like Hitler, he wanted to destroy them all—even the babies.

Haman is the creator of the crisis in the Book of Esther. He paid a fortune to make it happen. In fact, he offered the king two-thirds of the annual budget of Persia (Iran) to issue a decree that every Jewish man, woman, and child in the empire would be murdered in a single day. The entire tribe of Judah, marked for extermination—all because one Jewish man, Mordecai, refused to bow to Haman. Once sealed by the king, this royal decree could not be changed.

This is when Mordecai sends word to Esther with one of the most sobering messages in Scripture. He tells her plainly that if she remains silent, deliverance for the Jewish people will arise from another place—but she and her father's house will perish. Then he asks the question that is just as real today as it was then: "Who knows whether you have come to the kingdom for such a time as this?" (Est. 4:14, NKJV).

Esther had a choice. She could remain silent or risk everything. When Esther realized that silence was no longer an option, she did not rush forward impulsively. She did something far more significant: She asked the Jewish people to fast with her. Fasting strips away distraction and positions the heart to hear God clearly. Esther was about to step into a moment where favor alone would not be enough; she needed divine timing, divine strategy, and divine covering.

Approaching the king without being summoned was punishable by death. Esther knew the law. She knew the risk. And yet she also understood something deeper: Obedience to God sometimes places you in direct conflict with human systems. At that point, safety is no longer found in compliance but in surrender.

Her words in Esther 4:16 (NKJV), "If I perish, I perish," are not resignation. They are resolve. Esther was choosing obedience regardless of outcome. God's Glory rests on those who stop protecting themselves and start saying yes to Him.

This moment reveals the true cost of faithfulness to God's call. Esther could no longer rely on her position or her preparation alone. She had to trust God with the outcome.

The Glory Connection

For the church, this is a defining lesson. As Glory increases, moments will arise when our obedience carries visible risk. Standing with God's covenant purposes—especially concerning Israel—will not always feel safe or socially rewarded. That is why intercession must precede action. Without it, courage collapses under pressure.

Esther did not change the decree by protest. She confronted it by cooperating with God's strategy. And her obedience unlocked a reversal that no human could produce.

This is how Glory works. It does not remove risk but carries authority into it. And once Esther crossed that threshold, everything changed—not only for her but for an entire people.

This is where the Esther pattern reveals its end-time application. Church, this is why you were born. You were not placed in this generation by accident. Your destiny, your calling, is found in Romans 11:11: "Salvation has come to the Gentiles, to make them [the Jewish people] jealous." The apostle Paul is telling the Gentile church that your purpose is to cause the Jewish people to want to know the lover of their souls—the Messiah of Israel.

The Glory is coming, and the Jewish people are the key to its release. The Glory began with the Jewish people. The Messiah came through the Jewish people. And the Messiah will return to one nation on earth—Israel.

The Glory belongs to Israel. In Romans 9:4, Paul says that the Israelites are the ones "to whom belong the adoption, the glory, the covenants, the giving of the law, the service of God, and the promises." This echoes what the prophet Isaiah spoke: "I will grant salvation"—Yeshua—"in Zion, and My glory for Israel" (Isa. 46:13).

Here is the divine order: The Glory resting on Israel will trigger the greatest Jewish revival in history. And that revival will, in turn, release the greatest Gentile revival the world has ever seen.

And that is exactly what happens in the Book of Esther. When the Jewish people are spared, revival breaks out among the Gentiles.

Victory and Salvation

God is brilliant. Instead of canceling the decree, God released a higher strategy. The Jewish people were equipped with swords so they could defend themselves.

The sword represents the Word of God. The Word of God is *the most powerful weapon* on earth, in heaven, and in hell!

Esther's assignment was not to rescue the Jewish people by herself. It was to position them to stand, to fight, and to overcome. When the Jewish people were equipped, Scripture tells us they gained power over those who hated them. What was intended for their destruction became the means of their victory.

Something else happened that most people overlook. Revival broke out among the Gentiles. Esther 8:17 says that many people in the land professed to be Jews because the dread of the Jews fell upon them. Instead of killing the Jewish people, many converted because they saw God on the Jewish people.

That's what's about to happen in Israel now. Israel is about to be ablaze with the Glory of God.

In recent years, a great revival has been taking place in Iran. Iranians have been turning to Jesus in huge numbers. Millions of Christians who have come to know the Lord in

Iran are praying fervently to Him. When the recent strikes on Iran and its proxies got rid of an awful tyrant, the people of Iran were dancing in the streets. They were so happy.

I believe this will only continue as events unfold in the Middle East. I've talked to Iranians living in the United States, and I know how they're thinking. They need a rock. They need something stronger than themselves. And when they see the reality of God, many are responding—just like in the Book of Esther.

You see, God was all over the Book of Esther, even though His name was never mentioned. He was rearranging circumstances behind the scenes to preserve the Jewish people. And He is still doing that today.

Your Esther Moment

Mordecai told Esther if she stayed silent, deliverance for the Jewish people would still come from another place. In other words, God's covenant with the Jewish people would not fail, but Esther could miss her moment. God would still accomplish His purpose—but she would lose the privilege of being part of it.

That principle runs throughout Scripture. God's plans are secure, but individuals can miss their assignment.

And then Mordecai asked the question that echoes through history: "Who knows whether you have come to the kingdom for such a time as this?"

I believe the church is standing in that same moment today. God will fulfill His covenant promises to the Jewish people. That is certain. But the question facing the church is this: Will we recognize our moment and take our place in what God is about to do?

It's time to get ready for the greatest Jewish revival in history. And Romans 11:11 is your written invitation from God to participate.

> I say then, have they [the Jewish people] stumbled that they should fall? God forbid! But through their transgression, salvation has come to the Gentiles, to make them jealous.

So I ask you plainly: Are you a friend of God? The Glory of God is a two-edged sword. For God's friends, the Glory brings victory. For God's enemies, it brings dread. If you want to be a friend of God, you must know Him—not through ritual, not through religion, but through relationship.

Once you belong to Him, you are ready to receive what I call the Esther anointing, the Esther Glory. It carries favor, purity, destiny, and courage. It marks a sudden supernatural turning point in a person's life.

So I pray in Jesus' name: Receive the Esther Glory! Take up your sword. Speak the Word. Step into your Esther moment because you were born for this.

Chapter 13

ANTI-SEMITISM AND THE SPIRIT OF ANTICHRIST

How does a little nation like Israel get in the newspaper every single day? It happens because this small land the size of Rhode Island is important to God.

The attempt to wipe out the Jewish people is more than ignorance or prejudice. Anti-Semitism is a demonic spirit that opposes the King of the Jews Himself. And until the church recognizes it as spiritual, it will never be dealt with properly.

Remember God's promise, so bold that it leaves no room for ambiguity: As long as there is a sun, moon, and stars, there will be Jewish people on the earth (Jer. 31:35–36). That means every attempt to eliminate the Jews is an attempt to make the Bible look false. Satan understands this. And that is why he has never stopped trying.

To understand why anti-Semitism is spiritual warfare, you must understand how the enemy operates. Satan does not fight humanity at random. He resists whatever God is advancing in the earth at a given moment. Scripture is clear: God's redemptive plan is bound to His covenant with Israel.

From the beginning, the enemy's goal has been to stop this covenant. When God chose Abraham, opposition followed. When Israel multiplied in Egypt, Pharaoh moved toward extermination. When Messiah was born, Herod ordered the slaughter of Hebrew children.

I have lived long enough to know that this did not always look the way it does now, at least not in America. There was never a time when anti-Semitism didn't exist, but there was a time when it was not openly celebrated or casually excused.

Now, I'm an optimist. I don't tend to focus on the end of the world. But with current events in the Middle East, I'm beginning to see things speeding up pertaining to end-time prophecies. And I can actually see how the world could instantly become anti-Semitic with the way things are going.

It would be so easy for this to happen worldwide right now, as we saw it happen in Germany before the Holocaust. It's hard to believe a nation could normalize the slaughter of six million people, even after the fact. But I see the same spirit manifesting today in the United States and throughout the world.

America could easily fall into the anti-Semitism trap and become another Nazi-like nation. Why? Because it's a spiritual battle. Anti-Semitism is satanic. Demonic powers working through human agents come against Jewish people globally. Especially in Europe right now, more and more Jewish people are realizing they have no future in these countries and are looking to make their home in Israel.

What has changed since October 7, 2023, is the boldness of anti-Semitism. What used to stay hidden is now out in the open for everyone to see. In the wake of the worst massacre of Jewish people since the Holocaust, hostility toward Jewish people has surged across America—on college campuses and in public demonstrations. Jewish families who never imagined needing security now have to rethink their safety.

The Anti-Defamation League conducted a Global 100 survey in 2025. The results were that anti-Jewish sentiment is at an all-time high. It found that 46 percent of adults worldwide—that's 2.2 billion people—"harbor deeply entrenched anti-Semitic attitudes."[1] That number more than doubled in just ten years, compared with their first Global 100 survey in 2015.

And since the recent strikes against Iran and its proxies (in 2026), we have seen another huge upsurge of anti-Semitism. It's gone way beyond what we saw before. It's likely that in the wake of these strikes, more than half the world's population has become anti-Semitic or anti-Israel in their thinking.

Let the Holy Spirit Search Your Heart

I want to challenge those of you reading this book to let the Holy Spirit search your hearts. Allow Him to shine His light on anything you have excused, inherited, laughed at, ignored, or spiritualized away.

Some of you have never considered that anti-Semitism can be a spirit, not just an opinion. Others have recognized it in culture but never thought to confront it in a bloodline, a church environment, or a spiritual framework.

The purpose of this chapter is for you to get clean and live in "instant repentance." Ask the Lord, right now, to show you anything in your heart—any bias, any contempt, any apathy, any "I'm sure it doesn't matter" posture—that is not in keeping with His covenant heart. And when He shows you, renounce it. Repent. Break agreement with it. Because God is not trying to condemn you; He is trying to free you from a spirit that opposes the King of the Jews.

Anti-Semitism has survived every attempt to eliminate it. It adapts, changes language, and disguises itself. But its target never changes.

Israel stands at the center of God's redemptive timeline. The return of Messiah, the final harvest, and the restoration of all things are inseparably connected to what Scripture declares will take place among the Jewish people. And when that reality draws closer, resistance becomes louder.

Recognizing this does not minimize the pain anti-Semitism causes. It explains why it must be addressed spiritually, not just emotionally or politically. Rising hostility is not evidence that God's purposes are failing. It is evidence that they are advancing.

Scripture has already told us this would happen. And God has already shown us how to respond.

Instead of issuing statements and distancing ourselves from it publicly, we need to confront it spiritually. Until we do, it will keep resurfacing—even inside the church.

That means anti-Jewish jokes, attitudes, or doctrines cannot be brushed off as bias problems. They must be treated as deliverance issues. Churches need to build moments into their services where people repent—not just personally but corporately—for anti-Jewish attitudes in their bloodline and in their congregation.

Standing with Israel is having God's heart for the nation and the Jewish people and being on God's side in these last days of demonic deception. No one else is saying it this way—but it must be said.

You cannot be anti-Israel but not anti-Jewish. That is a false distinction. Israel, the Jewish people, and Zionism are biblically and historically interwoven. Every time a crisis erupts—Iran, Venezuela, New York, anywhere—someone finds a way to blame Zionists, Israel, or Jews. It makes no rational sense until you see it as spiritual.

If you're a Christian and anti-Israel, there's a disconnect in your spiritual identity. The "I'm just anti-Zionist" mask must be confronted. It is the same spirit.

Speaking of being anti-Zionist, I want you to know something. God is a Zionist. I am a Zionist. Every real Christian should be a Zionist. Even AI knows this.

I looked up the word *Zionism* using AI, and the definition was simple: It refers to the biblical belief that God promised the land of Israel to the Jewish people.

Do you know what anti-Israel or anti-Semitism is? It's a synonym for hating God.

You tell me you hate Zionism. You tell me you hate Jewish people. You tell me you hate Israel. Then you might as well finish the statement. You hate God. Why? The Bible tells us what God thinks about Israel and the Jewish people.

Once you know what God's Word says about the land, you understand that standing with Israel is not a political issue. It is a gospel issue. If you understand prophecy, you know that no matter what you see with your natural eye,

God has the last word. God's Word *is* the last word. So let's examine what His Word says about Israel.

The reason anti-Semitism never dies is not random hatred—it is a targeted spiritual campaign against a specific covenant. If you want to understand why the enemy never stops, you have to understand what he is trying to stop. And what he is trying to stop is God's fulfillment of the most specific, most repeated, and most legally binding promise in all Scripture—the land covenant. This is the prize. This is why the land is contested. This is why Jewish people are targeted. The enemy knows that if this covenant is fulfilled, his time is up.

In Amos 9:15 God is speaking, and He says, "I will plant them upon their land." That's the Jewish people upon the land of Israel. And He's saying, once I do this, "no more will they be uprooted out of their land which I have given them." Who gave them the land of Israel? God Himself. Once they returned, Israel became a nation in 1948, and in 1967, Jerusalem was once again in Jewish hands. Now that they have returned, no one is going to drive them out again, according to the Word of God.

When Tucker Carlson interviewed Mike Huckabee on February 20, 2026, it made headlines throughout the world because Tucker Carlson said that, according to the Bible, if the descendants of Abraham were to receive all the Promised Land today, it would essentially include the entire Middle East. Then he asked Huckabee whether Israel had a right to all that land. Huckabee responded, "It would be fine if they took it all."[2]

Well, the truth of the matter is, we don't have anywhere near the land that God promised the Jewish people. I say *we* because I'm Jewish, and I have dual citizenship. I'm Israeli as well as American.

And actually, my answer to who owns the land will surprise you.

God's Covenant with the Jewish People

God makes His position about the Jewish people very clear in Scripture.

First, He explains why Israel was chosen in the first place. Deuteronomy 7:7–8 says,

> The LORD did not set His love on you nor choose you because you were more in number than any of the peoples, for you were the fewest of all the peoples. But it is because the LORD loved you and because He kept the oath which He swore to your fathers.

Israel was chosen because of God's love and His covenant promise.

Then God says something even more remarkable. In Exodus 4:22 He tells Moses to say to Pharaoh, "Israel is My son, even My firstborn." There is something special about a firstborn child. God is saying that Israel holds a unique place in His heart.

And God makes it clear that He will never forget them. In Isaiah 49:15–16 He answers Israel's fear that they have been abandoned: "Can a woman forget her nursing child, and have no compassion on the son of her womb? Even these may forget, yet I will not forget. See, I have inscribed you on the palms of My hands."

Now, here is something that amazes me. According to the Bible, there is only one city in the world—only one city in history—where God actually promises a blessing if we pray for it. That's unbelievable. God almost bribes us to pray for this city with such a promise.

Psalm 122:6 says, "Pray for the peace of Jerusalem: 'May they prosper who love you!'"

Do you know what the word *peace* is in Hebrew? *Shalom*. But the deeper meaning of *shalom* is completeness. So the verse is really saying to pray for the completeness of Jerusalem.

I thank God that President Trump, the current president as I write this, understands the importance of standing with Israel because the United States and Jerusalem have to stay together for God's greatest blessing.

Psalm 122:6 continues: "May they prosper who love you!" If you pray for the peace of Jerusalem, you will prosper. But prosperity in the Hebrew sense is not just about money. Derek Prince, who I mentioned earlier, told me that the Hebrew idea behind the word *prosper* means something much deeper—it means heart peace.

So this verse is really saying: Pray for the completeness of Israel, and those who love Israel will have peace in their hearts.

The Bible reinforces this in Psalm 135:4: "For the LORD has chosen Jacob for Himself, and Israel for His special possession." Think about that. You may have possessions, but God says Israel is His special possession.

No wonder He also says in Genesis 12:3, "I will bless them who bless you [Israel], and curse him who curses you."

If you look at history, you can see that covenant unfolding before your eyes. God scattered the Jewish people. God preserved the Jewish people. God regathered the Jewish people. The prophet Ezekiel declares that after their regathering, God will cleanse them, give them a new heart, and put His Spirit within them. Then, as Yeshua promised, those who believe in Him will experience rivers of living water flowing from within.

THE GREAT JEWISH LEASE

So now we come to the question everybody asks: Who owns the land? Do the Jewish people own it? Do the Muslims own it? Does Hamas own it?

I want to explain something that many believers have never heard before. I call it the great Jewish lease. Yes, you heard me correctly—a lease.

Why do I say it's a lease? Because when you read the Bible carefully, you discover that the land of Israel ultimately belongs to God Himself. The Jewish people do not own it in the normal sense of the word. It has been leased to them, rooted in the unconditional, everlasting covenant between God and Abraham.

Leviticus 25:23 states it plainly: "The land shall not be permanently sold, for the land is Mine." God owns the land of Israel.

So if the land cannot be sold permanently, what does that mean? It means God remains the owner, and there is only one other option. It can be leased. And the Jewish people are the ones He has given the right to live there according to His covenant with Abraham.

This covenant states the terms of the lease, and it's recorded in Genesis 15:18:

> On that same day the LORD made a covenant with Abram, saying, "To your descendants I have given this land, from the river of Egypt to the great Euphrates River."

Notice something very important. God did not say Abram purchased the land. God said He gave it. And because the land ultimately belongs to God, no government, army, or international body has the authority to cancel what God established.

And who are Abram's descendants? The Jewish people. Look at the boundaries—from the river of Egypt all the way to the Euphrates River. That's a lot of land.

We see that God had already made the promise earlier in Genesis 12:5–7:

> Abram took...the people that they had acquired [the Jewish people]...and they...came to the land of Canaan....The LORD appeared to Abram and said, "To your descendants I will give this land."

So He has now said it twice. If God says something one time that should be enough. If He says it two times, you'd better pay attention.

When it comes to other nations, God uses their treatment of Israel to determine whether they will be blessed or cursed. In Joel 3:2 God says,

> I will gather all the nations, and bring them down to the Valley of Jehoshaphat. I will enter into judgment with them there regarding My people and My heritage Israel, whom they have scattered among the nations; they have also divided up My land.

Notice the issue. They divided up God's land. They took portions of the land God gave Israel and gave it to others.

Later, under Joshua's leadership of the Israelites, God repeats the territorial promise again. Joshua 1:4 says,

> From the wilderness and this Lebanon, as far as the great river, the River Euphrates, all the land of the Hittites, and to the Mediterranean Sea toward the setting of the sun will be your territory.

As I mentioned earlier, according to current estimates, Israel presently possesses only a tiny fraction of the land God promised Abraham's descendants. The world already gets upset with Israel over the land they have now. What will happen when they take full possession of everything God promised?

Now the length of the lease is spelled out in one of my favorite psalms.

Psalm 105:8–11 says,

> He remembers His covenant forever, the word that He commanded, to a thousand generations, that the

> covenant He made with Abraham, and His oath to Isaac, and confirmed to Jacob as a decree, and to Israel for an everlasting covenant, saying, "To you I will give the land of Canaan as the portion of your inheritance."

How long is the lease? Forever. And just in case someone missed the word *forever*, it says it is for a thousand generations. That's a pretty long time. And just in case someone missed that, the psalm says it is everlasting. That sounds just like forever to me.

When God says something once, you should listen. When He says it twice, you really should listen. When He says it three times, you definitely better listen!

Now God also said something else to the Jewish people. If they sinned, they would be scattered. Deuteronomy 28:64 says, "The LORD will scatter you among all the peoples, from one end of the earth to the other."

And that is exactly what happened. The Jewish people were scattered to the four corners of the earth. We were persecuted in nation after nation. And yet, despite being scattered and persecuted everywhere we went, the Jewish people survived. There should be no Jewish people alive today based on the level of persecution my people have endured—except for God.

Even the rebirth of Israel happened supernaturally. Isaiah 66:8 asks, "Who has heard such a thing? Who has seen such things? Shall the earth be made to give birth in one day? Shall a nation be born at once?"

And that is exactly what happened. On May 14, 1948, David Ben-Gurion proclaimed the establishment of the State of Israel, and in a single day, a nation was reborn.

I've also heard an interesting story about President Harry Truman, who played a crucial role in recognizing Israel as a nation at that time. There's a reason for that. He had a good Christian mother who taught him that Israel must be a Jewish nation and that those who bless Israel will be blessed. When Truman became president and had the opportunity to recognize Israel, he remembered what his mother had taught him. And he acted.

So when you step back and look at the whole picture, something becomes obvious. The survival of the Jewish people makes no sense naturally. Nation after nation tried to wipe us out, yet we are still here. Empires rose and fell, but Israel returned to the land exactly the way the Bible said it would.

That tells you something important: If God is the one preserving the Jewish people, then you can be sure there is also a spiritual force trying to stop them. Now you understand why anti-Semitism has never made rational sense—and never will, until you see it for what it is.

Behind the rising hatred and confusion surrounding Israel is something far deeper than politics. There is a spiritual force at work—one the Bible calls the spirit of the antichrist. To understand what is happening in our world, we have to understand that spirit, how it spreads deception, and why it has always set itself against the Jewish people.

The Spirit of the Antichrist

Anti-Semitism is more than just another issue people argue about. It's a prophetic sign. When you read the Bible, you see a pattern. Periods of growing hostility toward the Jewish people often appear during times of spiritual deception and rebellion against God.

And there's another connection: The same spirit that tries to erase Israel from God's plan eventually turns its attention to the Messiah Himself. Once Israel is pushed aside, the next step is to redefine who Jesus really is. This pattern isn't coincidence. It follows a spiritual cause and effect.

When Israel is removed from the story, Jesus is separated from His Jewish identity. Once that happens, His return loses its meaning. Why? Because a Messiah disconnected from Israel is no longer the Messiah of Scripture.

And that is precisely how the spirit of antichrist operates. It does not always begin by denying Jesus outright. It tries to redefine Him. It reshapes Him into a form that is no longer threatening to the status quo. And that is dangerous!

In 2 Thessalonians 2:10–13, Paul warns that God allows strong delusion to come upon those who do not receive a love of the truth. Notice what he does not say. He does not say they lacked information. He does not say they were ignorant or uneducated. He says they did not love the truth.

And that's where many people struggle. It's easy to agree with truth. It's much harder to love it enough to let it change you and to stick with it even when it costs something. Especially when it comes to Israel and God's covenant purposes.

Scripture shows a pattern. When people turn away from the truth of God's covenant with Israel, spiritual confusion soon follows. And once deception takes hold, it doesn't stop there. The picture of Messiah begins to change too. People reshape Him to fit what they are willing to accept. We see that happening in churches across America today.

The Bible shows us something about the way God works. First, He reveals what He is going to do, and then He looks for people who will believe Him and respond. The prophet Amos said it this way: God does nothing without first revealing His plans to His servants the prophets (Amos 3:7). But hearing what God says is not enough. Once God reveals something, He expects us to respond. That is especially true when it comes to Israel. When God begins to highlight something in His Word, He is asking His people to stand with Him.

In this season, God is bringing Israel back into focus in a powerful way. That is one reason many people feel unsettled right now. Something is changing. As God's Glory increases, people can no longer stay neutral about the things that matter to God.

And Israel matters to God.

Chapter 14

SHEEP AND GOATS

I'M EIGHTY-FIVE YEARS young, and I lived in an era in the United States when there was a relatively low level of anti-Semitism. I mean, as a child, I heard anti-Semitic jokes. I can remember the time I wanted to go to a nearby beach but couldn't. The reason was printed on a sign that read, "No Dogs or Blacks or Jews Allowed!" But overall, the culture of our country throughout my lifetime has been relatively supportive of Israel and the Jewish people.

But with everything happening in the Middle East right now, anti-Semitism is once again raising its ugly head all over the world, including here in America. It seems that with the advent of social media, everyone now has a voice. Everyone, at virtually no cost, has a network. All you need is a car and an iPhone. And I am seeing more anti-Jewish and anti-Israel voices come to the surface. Even movie stars, professional athletes, and politicians are seeing the Palestinian people as "David" and Israel as "Goliath." History proves it's just the opposite. Which fire will you pour oil on? The devil's fire of anti-Semitism or God's fire of the Holy Spirit?

The fates of Israel, the church, and America are connected to one thing: how we treat the Jewish people and the nation of Israel. There is a key prophecy about this in the Bible, and we are watching it unfold right now. I love prophetic words that happen right now, even when they're a warning. Because when God speaks, He means what He says.

And one of those prophecies is taking place before our eyes. It's the separation of the sheep and the goats that Jesus spoke about in Matthew 25:31–32:

> When the Son of Man comes in His glory, and all the holy angels with Him, then He will sit on the throne of His glory. Before Him will be gathered all nations, and He will separate them one from another as a shepherd separates his sheep from the goats.

Sheep, as animals, follow the shepherd. Goats, as animals, have a mind of their own. The judgment of the nations is based on the separation of sheep nations and goat nations. If you're for Israel, you're a sheep nation. If you're against Israel, you're a goat nation.

So what, exactly, is the single issue on which the nations will be judged? I'm glad you asked. The answer is found in Matthew 25:40, which says, "The King will answer, 'Truly I say to you, as you have done it for one of the least of these brothers of Mine, you have done it for Me.'" This is what the separation is over.

When you look up the word *brothers* in the Greek, it means those from the same womb or the same flesh. Do you know who the physical brothers of Jesus are? The Jewish people. When Jesus says, "these brothers of Mine," He is talking about the Jewish people.

Now I want you to understand something about this passage that many people miss entirely. Jesus is not speaking here in general terms about kindness to the poor or care for the needy, although those things matter to God. He is speaking in a very specific prophetic context. Matthew 25 is part of the Olivet Discourse, Jesus' most detailed teaching about the end times. He has just finished talking about the signs of His return, the ten virgins, and the parable of the talents. And now He turns to the judgment of nations. This is end-time teaching. The separation He describes is happening in our day, right now, as the age draws to a close.

And here is where that gets me. It is not doctrine. It is not church attendance. It is not how many miracles you witnessed or how many prophecies you gave. When Jesus separates the nations, He does it on one issue and one issue only: how they treated His Jewish brothers. That's it. Just that one thing.

I have heard people argue that Jesus was referring to all believers as His brothers in this passage. And I understand why they read it that way. But look at the context. Jesus is speaking to His Jewish disciples about what will happen at the end of the age. He has just come from the temple in Jerusalem. He is a Jewish rabbi speaking to Jewish followers about a coming judgment of Gentile nations. The natural reading of "these brothers of Mine" in that context is unmistakable. He is talking about the Jewish people, His physical family, His kinsmen according to the flesh. Paul uses the same language in Romans 9:3 when he speaks of his grief for his own people, calling them his "brothers" and his "kinsmen according to the flesh."

Yeshua identifies Himself so completely with the Jewish people that He says what is done to them is done to Him.

You cannot separate Jesus from Israel without distorting who He is. He was not born into a generic human family. He was born into a specific covenant people: the tribe of Judah, the line of David. His Jewishness is not incidental to His identity. It is central to it. And because it is central to His identity, how you treat His Jewish brothers is, in His own words, how you treat Him.

Those who curse the Jewish people and Israel will be cursed and spiritually blinded in this life and suffer in fire eternally if they don't repent (Matt. 25:41). But those who bless the Jewish people and Israel will be blessed in every area of their life, both now and at their final judgment.

The History Books Don't Lie

I want to show you something. Genesis 12:3 is not just a promise sitting in the Old Testament waiting to be applied someday. It has been applied throughout history. And if you know where to look, the pattern is impossible to miss.

Take Cyrus the Great. Here was a Persian king who had no reason, politically or personally, to care about the Jewish people. And yet God moved on his heart, and he issued a decree allowing the Jewish exiles to return to their land and rebuild the temple in Jerusalem. Isaiah actually prophesied about Cyrus by name two hundred years before he was born. And what happened to Cyrus? He became the most powerful ruler on earth. His empire stretched from the Mediterranean to India. He is remembered to this day as one of the greatest leaders in human history. You bless the Jewish people; you get blessed. It's that simple.

Now look at Britain. In 1917, the British government issued the Balfour Declaration, officially supporting the establishment of a national home for the Jewish people in the land of Israel. Britain was at the height of its global power. But then something shifted. In 1939—just as the Jewish people in Europe were facing the Holocaust—Britain issued the White Paper, dramatically restricting Jewish immigration to Palestine and effectively slamming the door shut on Jewish refugees who had nowhere else to go. Within a decade, the British Empire began its rapid and irreversible decline. I am not saying that is the only reason. History is complicated. But I am saying the timing is worth noticing.

And then there is the United States. President Harry Truman recognized the State of Israel just eleven minutes after it declared independence in 1948, against the advice of almost everyone around him, including his own secretary of state. He did it because, as he later said, he had a Christian mother who taught him the Bible. He knew what God said about the Jewish people, and he acted on it. And America? America went on to experience the greatest period of prosperity and global influence in its history. Coincidence? I don't think so.

Now contrast that with what happened to nations that went the other way. Egypt. Babylon. The Roman Empire. Nazi Germany. The Spanish Empire, which expelled every Jewish person from its territory in 1492, the same year that Columbus sailed west and Spain began losing the very dominance it thought it was protecting. These were not small nations with limited reach. They were the most powerful empires of their day. And every single one of them that set itself against the Jewish people ended up on the ash heap of history.

God is not subtle about this. He said what He meant in Genesis 12:3, and He has been proving it for four thousand years.

The Question Being Asked Right Now

October 7 was a spiritual alarm clock. Matthew 25 is no longer just something to preach and teach about. The question is being asked in real time: Are you a sheep or a goat?

There is a powerful warning in Zechariah 2:8 (NASB 1995): "For thus says the LORD of Hosts: 'After glory He has sent me against the nations which plunder you, for he who touches you, touches the apple of His eye.'"

I want to stop on that phrase for a moment, "the apple of His eye." In Hebrew, the word *ishon*, translated as "apple," literally means "the little man."[1] It refers to the tiny reflection of yourself you see when you look closely into someone's eye. It is a picture of the pupil: the most sensitive, most exposed, most carefully protected part of the entire human body. You can cover almost every part of your body and protect it from harm. But your eye is always vulnerable, always exposed to the world around it. God is saying that is how He feels about the Jewish people. They are not one concern among many to Him. They are the most sensitive place in His heart.

And then He says whoever touches them touches that place.

Anti-Israel rhetoric—whether in churches, on campuses, or in casual conversation—is not harmless. You are not just talking about a country or expressing a political opinion. You are putting your finger directly into the most sensitive place in God's heart. I have a godly fear for any person or nation that does that because God takes it personally in a way that very few things in Scripture describe.

Think about what happens when someone pokes you in the eye. It doesn't matter how small the finger or how casual the gesture. The response is immediate and involuntary. Your whole body reacts. That is the image God chose to describe His relationship to the Jewish people. And you have to be pretty foolish to poke your finger in God's eye.

Any Gentile Christian who is wrong about Israel is dangerously close to being an enemy of God. This is not just about nations or political debates happening somewhere else. This is personal. How you respond to the Jewish people matters to God. He takes personally what happens to His covenant people.

Jesus made one thing very clear: Neutrality is not an option. There is no category in His teaching for people or nations who stay on the sidelines, no place for observers who say they'd rather not get involved. This does not mean believers have to become loud, angry, or confrontational. It's about the direction you move when the Glory of God increases: either toward God's purposes or away from them. To follow Yeshua on His terms means His priorities become your priorities. It doesn't mean "I follow Yeshua, but I do it my way." If Yeshua's heart is focused on Israel, His disciples must be too.

In His mercy, God reveals where we stand before judgment, not after it. He exposes the heart while there is still time to repent. That is not condemnation. That is grace. Nations, institutions, churches, and individuals are revealing where they stand through their actions right now. The dividing line is not Democrat or Republican, liberal or conservative. It comes down to one thing: Israel.

And that dividing line is appearing inside the church as well. I want to be honest and candid with you about what I am seeing. I have been in ministry for more than fifty years, and I have never seen such a clear separation forming among people who all call themselves believers. On one side, there are believers whose love for the Jewish people is deepening. They are praying more. They are giving more. They are speaking up when it would be easier to stay quiet. They are asking God how they can be part of what He is doing in Israel right now. And on the other side are believers who are drifting, quietly accommodating the world's narrative about Israel, softening their convictions, finding theological reasons to stay neutral, or worse, finding theological reasons to stand against Israel. And the gap between these two groups is widening every single month.

This is what I mean when I talk about the separation of the Greater Glory. As Glory increases, it does not make everyone in the room more comfortable. It makes things more distinct. It separates light from darkness, just as it did in Genesis 1. Jesus said those who believe in Him will do the works He did, and even greater works. But at the same time, the Bible says those who practice evil will become more evil. That contrast, the simultaneous increase of both, is the hallmark of the Greater Glory season. And we are living in it right now.

I believe the church is about to see things it has never seen before: miracles, healings, supernatural harvests of souls, signs and wonders that cannot be explained away. But I also believe that the same season will expose what has been hidden in hearts for a long time. The Glory of God is not only the Presence of God but also the light of God. And light, by its nature, reveals.

The history books have already shown us how this ends for nations. The only question that remains is a personal one: Which side of that line will you be on?

Chapter 15

THE JEWISH AWAKENING

Sometimes God speaks a word and waits one or two thousand years before fulfilling it. But when the time comes, let every man be a liar and God's Word be true.

Romans 11:26 states without qualification, "And so all Israel will be saved." I take that verse literally. When it says all Israel will be saved, it means *all* Israel—not partially, not symbolically, not metaphorically. And at some point, you also must decide whether you believe God means what He says.

Can you imagine a nation that will be totally saved? That's what God is saying.

Do you know how many other nations He says that about in the Bible? Zero. None. Not one. The Jewish nation, Israel, is the only nation and people group promised 100 percent salvation! This will be for all Jewish people living in Israel during that end-time event. They will instantly become believers.

That is not a small detail somewhere in the Bible. It sits at the very center of Paul's teaching about the faithfulness of God. And from the time I first became a believer, this promise grabbed hold of my heart. It has shaped my life and my calling ever since.

My urgent concern is for those Jewish people who will die without knowing Messiah Jesus before that great event. Not only is it my calling to reach them, but I believe it is the calling of the church in this hour. The Bible also shows us something many people overlook. Before that final moment, something begins to unfold: A veil lifts, and scales fall from Jewish eyes.

Life from the Dead

Paul uses language in Romans 11:15 that leaves no room for understatement. He says Israel's awakening will be "life from the dead." I don't believe he chose those words casually.

Resurrection is God reversing what appeared final. That matters because it tells us how Israel's awakening will unfold. What was closed opens. What was dormant responds. What looked finished begins again.

And there is something else Paul makes clear: This awakening is not just individual. It is collective. God is not describing isolated Jewish believers discovering Messiah one at a time—though that is happening and will continue. He is describing a people awakening together. Covenant memory returning. Identity restored.

I have met Jewish believers whose encounter with Messiah was so sudden and undeniable that it felt less like persuasion and more like awakening from sleep. In fact, that is my own story!

And resurrection never ends with the one who is raised.

When Jesus rose from the dead, the impact did not stay at the empty tomb. It released witness. It altered the trajectory of the world. In the same way, Israel's awakening will not terminate with Israel. It will release momentum that accelerates the gospel among the nations.

And that right there is why Paul connects Israel's fullness to what happens across the entire world! "Life from the dead" is not just a phrase. It is an expectation that something will wake up! And where there was nothing but resistance, the harvest is coming in!

I have a Jewish ministry, and I love telling the underdogs about Jesus. I say Jewish people are underdogs because most Christians don't share Jesus with them. They love the Jewish people, and that's good. But if Jewish people don't know the gospel, it's not true love if you don't tell them about it.

I've seen this principle proven firsthand in my own ministry. When we shifted toward Iranian Muslim evangelism, we quickly discovered that there's a world of difference between saying you love someone and actually sharing the good news. Once we began sharing the gospel with Muslims, the response was extraordinary. They are among the most spiritually open people in the world right now. That experience deepened my conviction: You cannot love people and hold back the gospel from them at the same time.

What God is about to do through Israel is the ignition of its final phase. Israel's awakening is a turning point with global consequences. The end of the age does not revolve around America, Rome, or any denomination. It revolves around Jerusalem.

When Israel awakens to Messiah, Jewish believers will rise not only as recipients of revelation but as witnesses—first to their own people and then to the nations. In that moment, the circuit God established from the beginning will be completed. Jesus tied His return to Israel's response, not the church's comfort (Matt. 23:39).

As a Christian, you should care deeply about this. Your faith rests on a Jewish story, a Jewish Messiah, Jewish apostles, a Jewish covenant that has never been revoked, and a Jewish return.

If you're exhausted and just trying to survive, that's exactly why you should care because God did not design the church to limp to the finish line alone—He designed it to be revived by Israel's awakening (Rom. 11:15). Without the Jew-first pattern, the church loses its root, its prophetic clarity, its identity, and its urgency. What remains may still look spiritual, but it no longer carries the weight of God's purpose.

The devil isn't threatened by a church with polished services or well-produced worship. He's terrified of a church that reconnects to the root that birthed it because that's where resurrection power flows, covenant is restored, and the purposes of God move forward.

The Arc of Full Return

God's redemptive plan is not complete until two things happen: Israel returns to Messiah, and Messiah returns to Israel. These two movements are inseparable. They are not parallel ideas; they are mirrored realities, each triggering the other.

Scripture reveals that the return of Messiah is not only a heavenly event, but it is a covenantal response. Heaven is waiting on earth. The Messiah waits for a people prepared to receive Him, and Israel waits for the unveiling of the One who was promised to her from the beginning. When these two returns meet, history reaches its appointed conclusion.

1. Gospel to Israel, then to the nations

Paul summarizes the present age with a prophetic order: "to the Jew first, and also to the Greek" (Rom. 1:16). The gospel went first to the Jew, then to the Gentile. That order was never accidental, and it was never revoked. Scripture reveals that what began that way will return that way.

This was never about favoritism. It is about God's supernatural, eternal law of evangelism.

God does not abandon His order because history becomes complicated. And when Israel awakens, the momentum released will move outward—touching nations, stirring harvest, and accelerating what God has always intended to bring to completion.

Israel is the root. Israel is the covenant carrier. Israel was called to be the original witness nation. And when Israel largely rejected the gospel, something happened that Paul describes with stunning clarity: Israel's stumbling opened the door for salvation to go to the nations (Rom. 11:11).

That shift initiated the church age, where Gentile believers carried Israel's Messiah to the world. But Paul is careful to stress that this was never the end of the story.

2. Nations make Israel jealous

Paul then describes a second movement, one that unfolds at the end of the age. He writes that "salvation has come to the Gentiles, to make [Israel] jealous" (Rom. 11:11). The goal was never replacement—it was provocation.

The result of that provocation is national awakening: "And so all Israel will be saved" (Rom. 11:26). This is not just individual salvation. It is covenantal restoration. Israel's return becomes a trigger event—releasing resurrection life not only to Israel but to the nations.

The Full Return Requires Two Acknowledgments

For Messiah to return, Scripture reveals that two acknowledgments must take place.

First, Israel must acknowledge Him. Jesus Himself prophesied this with precision: "You shall not see Me again until you say, 'Blessed is He who comes in the name of the Lord' " (Matt. 23:39). That statement is corporate, and it is eschatological. Jerusalem must welcome Him.

Second, the nations must honor Israel's role. Paul warns Gentile believers directly: "Do not boast against the branches....The root sustains you" (Rom. 11:18). End-time revival requires the nations to honor Israel's calling, Israel's covenant, and Israel's witness. Without Israel's return, the circuit remains incomplete.

The Prophets Saw This Return

The prophets consistently describe a future where a restored Jewish group becomes a witness to the nations. Zechariah sees the day when "ten men from every language of the nations will take hold of the garment of a Jew, saying, 'Let us go with you, for we have heard that God is with you' " (Zech. 8:23). Isaiah declares, "For out of Zion shall go forth the law, and the word of the Lord from Jerusalem" (Isa. 2:3).

This mirrors the apostolic pattern—now reappearing at the end of the age—and culminates in the return of Jesus to Jerusalem. Zechariah says His feet will stand on the Mount of Olives (Zech. 14:4). John writes that every eye will see Him, even those who pierced Him (Rev. 1:7).

Jewish-person-first eschatology is full-return eschatology. It envisions the day when Israel returns to Messiah, the nations return to Israel's calling, and the Messiah returns to Jerusalem.

Awakening Follows a Divine Pattern

There is a pattern in Scripture that most believers never notice until it unfolds in real time.

Whenever God moves to reach the nations, He begins with the Jewish people—not because He loves them more, but because He designed covenant to flow outward from them.

When God chose to bless the world, He began with one Jewish man—Abraham. When salvation entered history, it came through a Jewish Messiah.

And the pattern did not stop there.

Did you know that every major event in modern-day Israel's history has resulted in a major move of God's Spirit? First the natural, then the supernatural. Paul explains this in 1 Corinthians 15:46 (NKJV): "The spiritual is not first, but the natural, and afterward the spiritual." God has proven this principle in recent history.

The first Zionist Conference triggered the Azusa Street revival. When Israel became a nation in 1948, the great healing revival broke out. When Israel regained possession of Jerusalem in 1967, it opened the door for the Charismatic revival and the Jesus movement. And right after the Yom Kippur War in 1973, a revival among Jewish people gave birth to the modern Messianic Jewish movement.

These were not coincidences. They were previews.

Now fast-forward to more recent history. During the Jesus movement, from the late 1960s through the early 1970s, a powerful revival swept across the United States and eventually around the world. Young people were being saved by the thousands. Baptisms were taking place in oceans and rivers. Churches were being filled with a new hunger for the Presence of God.

But something else was happening inside that revival. Large numbers of young Jewish people began discovering that Yeshua was their Messiah. For the first time in centuries, Jewish believers in Jesus were emerging publicly and boldly declaring their faith. And these believers didn't simply "join" Christianity—they helped reform it and jolted a compromising church back to holiness and discipleship. I have witnessed it firsthand as first-century supernatural power returned through Jewish believers who were hungry not for religion but for encounter.

For example, Moishe Rosen encountered Jesus as the Messiah and went on to found Jews for Jesus, an evangelistic movement that has brought the gospel to Jewish communities around the world. Keith Green, a Jewish believer whose dramatic encounter with Jesus completely changed the direction of his life, became one of the most passionate prophetic voices of that generation. Marty Goetz and Paul Wilbur helped awaken the church to worship the God of

Israel and rediscover the biblical roots of our faith. And Art Katz—transformed from a searching intellectual into a prophetic teacher—became a powerful voice calling the church to repentance, holiness, and a deeper understanding of God's purposes for Israel in the last days. Leaders like Jonathan Bernis carried the gospel into Jewish communities around the world—particularly in Russia—while Martin Chernoff helped lead and shape the Messianic Jewish Alliance, strengthening the identity and witness of Jewish believers in Yeshua. And these are only a few. Too many Messianic Jewish pioneers to mention!

A revival that began almost sixty years ago is still shaping the Gentile church today through the lives of Jewish believers who discovered their Messiah during that awakening. Recently, someone said something to me that made me stop and think. They said, "Sid, isn't it interesting that God used a Jewish man to train the Gentile church in the supernatural and how to experience God?" I had never thought about it that way before. But it's true.

Personally, I do not call myself a Christian. I am a Christian by the literal definition of the word, but today the word has been redefined as someone who is not Jewish. As I wrote earlier, I was born a Jew, and I will die a Jew! I am a Jewish believer in the Jewish Messiah, Jesus!

Today, younger Jewish voices are shaping how a new generation understands worship, prophecy, and revival. God designed it this way because He knew something we are only beginning to rediscover: When the Jewish people are awakened to their Messiah, something accelerates in the spirit realm that reaches far beyond Israel itself.

The church has often misunderstood this sequence, assuming it was temporary or historical. But Scripture never presents it that way. It presents it as a pattern—one that reemerges whenever God moves on a global scale.

Jewish believers have repeatedly helped restore the church's holiness, worship, theology, mission, and power. And if this is what God has done through a remnant—through one generation here and another there—then imagine the day when all Israel awakens. That will be more than revival. It will be the full return, and it will shake the entire world.

A Lifetime Anchored in the Promise

I was born on September 7, 1940. As I mentioned earlier, I am now eighty-five years old. And at this stage of life, perspective changes. You stop defining success the way the world defines it. The question that matters is very simple: Did I do what God asked me to do?

I relate deeply to Caleb in the Bible in many ways. Caleb entered his inheritance at eighty-five. And what was his inheritance? Israel. He was given a specific portion of the land—Hebron, the place where Abraham, Isaac, and Jacob were buried.

Hebron represents legacy, covenant, and continuity. Caleb did not inherit something new. He stepped into something promised long before. His age did not disqualify him; it qualified him. He carried the faithfulness of God across generations.

When God brings an assignment to fulfillment, it is never early and never late. It arrives when the vessel can carry it without distortion. That is why this moment matters. Not because of my age but because of my readiness. It's not personal legacy or recognition I'm after—it is the fulfillment of my assignment. God does not preserve life without purpose.

I can honestly say that the purpose of my life has not yet even started. If that's true for me, and it is, how much more for you!

One of the great misconceptions about testimony is that it exists only for the moment in which it is given. Scripture presents a very different picture. Testimony is not consumed when it is shared; it is stored.

For decades, stories of healing, deliverance, and supernatural encounter were shared faithfully through our broadcasts—sometimes celebrated, sometimes dismissed, sometimes misunderstood. But none of them were wasted. Each one was a witness, not only to those who heard it at the time, but to a future moment when accumulated testimony would carry authority beyond explanation.

When the Glory increases, testimonies—including Jewish testimonies—will become the catalyst for revival. They awaken hunger and prepare the ground for a harvest that words alone could never produce.

I have been doing this for fifty-five years, and, as of now, not one year has been wasted.

The Role of the Church

Throughout history, righteous Gentiles have played a quiet but decisive role in the preservation and awakening of the Jewish people. In times of crisis, when Jewish lives were threatened or marginalized, those who stood with them did so in remarkably consistent ways. They prayed for Jewish people. They bore witness to Jewish people. And they gave—supporting those who were called to reach Jewish people.

The Gentile church is not called to replace Israel, speak over Israel, or distance itself from Israel. It is called to stand alongside God's covenant purposes with humility and faithfulness. The church's role is not domination, correction, or detachment. It is provocation—not through argument but through a lived relationship with God.

Paul describes this clearly when he speaks of provoking Israel to jealousy. That jealousy is not stirred by pressure or persuasion. It is stirred when Jewish people encounter Gentile believers who walk in authentic relationship with the God of Abraham, Isaac, and Jacob—believers whose lives are marked by Glory that cannot be explained away.

Going to the Jew first is not outdated. It is not a strategy tied to one era or one ministry. It is eternal order. What God established at the beginning, He does not abandon at the end.

The Harvest That Prepares the Way

When the Jewish people turn to their Messiah in large numbers, it will release a worldwide move of God unlike anything we have ever seen. Think about it this way: If a few thousand Jewish believers discovering their Messiah during the Jesus movement helped ignite spiritual hunger across the church, what will happen when Israel itself is set ablaze with the Glory of God?

Imagine thousands of Israeli Jewish believers filled with the Holy Spirit and operating in the Glory of God. Imagine miracles, signs, and wonders flowing through them just as we saw in the Book of Acts. When the Glory comes, Jerusalem will once again become the epicenter of a worldwide awakening. The fire of God will spread from Israel to the nations just as it did in the beginning—only this time it will be far greater.

The Book of Acts was the first spark. The Jesus movement was another spark. But when the Glory comes to Israel, the greatest harvest in human history will begin.

As Israel awakens, life from the dead spreads outward. What begins as recognition becomes testimony. What begins as testimony becomes harvest. Nations are gathered. Glory increases. And the earth moves closer to the moment Scripture has promised from the beginning.

I'm not writing this to give you optimism. I'm trying to give you certainty. God has spoken. God is faithful. And all Israel shall be saved.

We are not waiting for this awakening to begin. We are living at its threshold.

Chapter 16

RETURNING TO THE BEGINNING

Messianic Vision, which I founded as a radio show in 1977, was never a natural ministry. It was never built by strategy, trend, or human planning. I was led step by step, often without knowing where the next step would lead. Looking back now, I can see that God was preparing me. That is what the last fifty-plus years have really been about.

Everything God has emphasized—every encounter, every restoration of the supernatural, every season of preparation—has been leading toward one reality: Greater Glory. The manifest Presence of God is a reality that shapes my very life.

What God is doing in this hour is a return to something He made unmistakably clear at the beginning because it is required now more than ever.

From the very start, my calling was simple: Reach Jewish people with the gospel.

Before television. Before global platforms. Before conferences, books, and audiences. Before anyone knew my name, I knew why God had apprehended me. He had revealed Himself to me as Messiah, and He had placed an unrelenting burden in my heart for my own people.

Everything that came afterward grew out of that calling.

THE ORDER THAT GOVERNS THE GOSPEL: THE LAW OF EVANGELISM

Some have expressed amazement at how easily I lead people to the Lord. Wherever I go, I find that the unsaved are receptive to the good news. I pray this book will equip you to move supernaturally in this same gift. Always remember that anything I can do, you can do better. My ceiling can be your floor!

Many Bible believers know the spiritual laws about healing. Many also know the spiritual laws of prosperity. Both are valid and important. But you can't take your money to heaven. And you won't need healing in heaven. The only thing you take to heaven is souls! This is why Proverbs 11:30 says, "He who wins souls is wise."

I have found that most believers do not know that there is also a law of evangelism.

Paul states plainly in Romans 1:16, "For I am not ashamed of the gospel of [Messiah]. For it is the power of God for salvation to everyone who believes, to the Jew first, and also to the Greek." Paul was revealing an order that still governs how the gospel moves. And order matters.

If I create evangelistic literature to reach Gentiles, I will reach very few Jewish people. But when I design evangelistic materials to reach Jewish people, I will reach multitudes of Gentiles as well. I have found that I reach more Gentiles by going to the Jew first than by going to the Gentile first! This is the law of evangelism.

Using Every Means Necessary

When God gives an assignment, He also provides the means to fulfill it.

Reaching Jewish people both in Israel and throughout the nations requires persistence. That is why I am committed to using every means available: television, radio, digital media, outreach, and personal witness. This is not about visibility. It is about saturation. The message must go where the people are.

Many Jewish people will never walk into a church. Some will never attend a public meeting. But they will watch. They will listen. They will consider. Seeds are planted quietly, often long before they are acknowledged, and sometimes long before fruit becomes visible.

At eighty-five years old, many people are thinking about slowing down. I am thinking about finishing well. Not by doing less but by doing what matters most.

And I want something for you too—not for "someday," not for the version of you that has more time, more energy, or fewer complications. I want you to finish well.

Finishing well is not about doing more; it's about doing what matters most. It's about letting God bring you back to your first love—back to what He told you, back to what He emphasized, back to the assignments you delayed because other things felt urgent. My first love has always been the salvation of Israel.

If God is stirring you while you read this, don't brush it off. That stirring is often the beginning of God leading you into something He wants you to do.

God continues to show me what remains to be done. And as I respond, He continues to supply strength for it.

I may be eighty-five, but the calling has not diminished. It has intensified.

Why This Moment Matters

If you've read this far in the book, you've gotten the point that Jewish evangelism is not a side mission. It is central to God's redemptive plan. The gospel began in Israel. It went to the nations. And it will return to Israel. Everything in history is returning to Jerusalem.

This is why returning to the beginning matters. If you don't start where God started, the end-time harvest won't make sense. But when you return to the beginning, everything comes into focus.

For us at Messianic Vision, this isn't just an idea. It shapes everything we do. It defines where our resources go, how we measure fruit, and what we prioritize in our assignment.

When God begins to increase the harvest, He also calls people to be ready. (See Matthew 9:37–38.) When God draws near, He does not leave us as we are. His Presence always brings a moment of decision: You either move toward Him, or you hold back. You either obey, or you delay. Many people are waiting for more clarity when God is waiting for obedience.

So the real question is not what God is doing. The real question is this: Who is willing to move with Him? God is shaking everything that can be shaken so that His people will stand firm when it matters most.

Redefining "Normal"

It is time to redefine what "normal" looks like in our churches. When I read the history of the first church in the Book of Acts, I am provoked to jealousy. Being a "normal" believer meant healing the sick, casting out demons, raising the dead, hearing from God, speaking in supernatural languages, and seeing your prayers answered.

Somewhere along the way, expectations shifted. The culture, leadership style, and power of the church changed. We stopped being normal. And as a result, fewer and fewer Jewish people came to faith.

Heaven measures normal very differently from today's church. God is not satisfied with occasional salvations. He is saying plainly, "A church without a regular harvest is abnormal."

Ask God to connect you to the harvest He has already prepared. Not just the already-churched but local Jewish people, immigrants, refugees, young people, successful Jewish people, and retired Jewish people—those who are searching, even if they do not yet know what they are searching for. The harvest is closer than we think, but it requires us to lift our eyes beyond familiarity and comfort.

Invite the Glory of God into your life—and into your church. When you encounter His Glory, everything changes. Your posture changes. Your priorities change. Your direction changes. The Glory reveals who is willing to move from believing to a relationship where you truly know Him. We can't continue to define normal Christians as people who prayed a prayer. We have to start asking ourselves whether they truly came to know Him.

If the church does not redefine what normal looks like right now, we will keep mistaking activity for obedience and comfort for fruit.

Encounter Is No Longer Optional

Agreement with truth in your mind is not the same thing as being changed by that truth. You can believe all the right things about God and still not know God in a real way.

Salvation is not the finish line. It is the starting line. When someone prays a prayer to receive Jesus, that is the start of the journey. If it doesn't lead to an encounter with God, discipleship, and real transformation, we end up with churches full of sincere but unprepared people.

Billy Graham said he would rather make disciples than converts. Why? He knew that most people who respond to an altar call and pray a simple prayer will backslide a month later or a week later.

But the truth is that most people—unless they have one ingredient—will not pay the price to become a disciple, even if they went forward to say a prayer of salvation. What is that ingredient? The gospel demands it: experiential knowledge.

When you experience His Presence and feel Him tangibly in the room, you know that He's real. I could never deny God because I had experienced God.

Your experience will be different from mine, but it's what you need. Perhaps you prayed a prayer once or grew up believing in God because that's what your parents believed.

But if you're honest right now, you'll admit you've never had experiential knowledge of God.

A borrowed faith will collapse when life gets heavy. But when you have experienced God for yourself, something settles deep inside you.

There is an old saying that is still true today: A man with an experience is never at the mercy of a man with an argument. When you have encountered God for yourself, no argument can talk you out of what you know.

That is why the Holy Spirit is not optional in the life of a believer; He is essential.

And speaking in tongues is not strange or fringe. It is a gift from God, a love language shared with Him. It strengthens your spirit and keeps your heart sensitive to His Presence. It fuels what I call the Glory life—a life lived aware of God, expecting Him to move, and walking closely with Him.

God is calling the church into deeper relationship, into holiness, and into a real life shaped by His Presence.

We need to know more than the language of faith. We need to know the strength of faith built on experience. He calls us not just to learn truth but to know Him—the One who is the Truth.

This is why I believe God is pressing the church now to go deeper with Him. Because the people who truly know Him will recognize His voice when it matters most. And an encounter with God is not just for our personal comfort. It prepares us to help others be ready for what is coming.

An Invitation

All these things I'm pointing out to you come from what God has been dealing with in my own heart and ministry. I'm not asking you to do anything that I haven't already asked of myself. I am inviting you to align your heart with what God is doing.

That invitation is very practical.

You can pray. You can give. You can share your testimony. You can love Jewish people enough to tell them the truth about their Messiah. Those choices place you inside what God is doing right now.

Chapter 17

GLORY, HARVEST, AND THE RETURN OF MESSIAH

WHETHER THE WORLD acknowledges it or not, Israel sits at the center of what God is doing in the earth. This is why Israel remains such a point of contention. It is not because the land is large or strategically valuable but because it is spiritually decisive. What happens there reverberates everywhere else.

That is also why crisis so often converges on Israel. When fires break out, when wars intensify, and when hostility escalates, it is tempting to stop and lament. But lament is not the final word. The enemy always counterfeits before God fulfills. What we are seeing in the natural is a twisted echo of what is coming in the Spirit.

The last fire over Israel will not be destruction. It will be the fire of the Holy Spirit. Israel will burn—not with rocket but with revival.

I see Israel ablaze with the Presence of God. I see the greatest awakening in history beginning there. I see Israeli believers—on fire with the Spirit—going out to the nations, carrying the message of Messiah with authority and boldness. The same land that first received the gospel will send it again, not as history repeated but as history completed.

This is why everything converges here—the increase of Glory, the acceleration of harvest, the exposure of deception. They all meet in Israel.

God is not improvising. He is finishing what He began. The gospel started in Israel, went to the nations, and will return to Israel—not to circle backward but to bring the story to its appointed conclusion.

This is why the church cannot afford to treat Israel as a side issue or a sentimental cause. Israel is not an add-on to the gospel story. It is woven into its structure. To misunderstand Israel is to misunderstand where history is headed.

The shaking we see now is not random. It is purposeful. It's important to keep up with what's happening in the Middle East because, in the end times, everything focuses on the nation of Israel. God is aligning the earth for what comes next, and Israel stands at the center.

The question is not whether Israel will play a role. That has already been decided. The question is whether the church will recognize the moment while there is still time to move with it.

A Prophetic Window Is Open Now

There are moments in history when timing itself becomes a message. This is one of those moments.

God does not move randomly. Throughout the Bible, He works within appointed times—moments when He calls

His people to respond. When God highlights a season, it is His way of saying, "Pay attention. Move with Me."

The number seven has always spoken of completion, wholeness, and God's perfect work. When that number is repeated, it signals strength added to completion—a reinforcement of what God has already established. This is not superstition. It is a pattern. God uses time to emphasize purpose.

As I write this, Israel's seventy-seventh anniversary is upon us. It's significant, but not because of a year or a date on the calendar. I believe this places us in a marked season for Israel—an appointed moment that carries unusual weight. It launches a season of strengthened covenant and completed gaps—both for Israel and for those who are grafted into Israel's story. What God has preserved, He is now fortifying.

I believe this window carries a promise of strength—strength for Israel and strength for those who bless Israel. Strength to stand. Strength to obey. Strength to finish well. It is an invitation into wholeness: in body, in calling, in family, and in purpose.

But prophetic windows do not remain open indefinitely. When God signals His timing, He is inviting His people to move before circumstances force the issue. I believe right now we are in a season where God is compressing the end times. Things in the Middle East are accelerating, and the pace has quickened.

In a live interview I did with my good friend Barry Segal on March 10, 2026, he put it this way: "Israel is God's [prophetic] time clock." And he believes that the events of October 7 caused "a quantum shift inside the prophetic timetable of what God is doing right now in the earth. And that's why we're seeing not just wars and rumors of wars, but in Israel, I can tell you nearly every year through the past several years...Israel has been at war as a nation."[1] The bottom line is that we need to share the truth about Yeshua with everyone we can while there is still time.

All Eyes on the Temple Mount

In my interview with Barry, we talked about the significance of Psalm 83 and Ezekiel 38–39. If people would take the time to study these chapters, they would begin to see something remarkable.

Barry talked about how these two prophecies look like layers of prophetic tracing paper laid one over the other, the way architects layer plans. Psalm 83 describes God rising in His fury. Then the picture transitions into the great war described in Ezekiel 38–39. That war will happen. It's not speculation.

I believe the outcome of the recent strikes on Iran (in 2026) and its proxies will be a time when millions of Iranians and others in the Middle East have an opportunity to respond to God's love and a remnant is gathered. Regardless of when you read this book, one thing is clear: Any time we watch what is happening in Israel and the Middle East, we are watching God's prophetic Word unfold in real time.

If you asked me where we are between the news headlines and Scripture, I would say we are somewhere in the midst of Psalm 83, moving toward Ezekiel 38–39. And the transition is happening rapidly.

Barry shared something else with me that I have not been able to get out of my mind. He said, "I really believe all eyes right now are on Israel, the Middle East, and especially the Temple Mount in Jerusalem. I had a disturbing dream recently. I couldn't shake it. The thought kept coming back to me: What about the Temple Mount?

"That mountain belongs to the God of Abraham, Isaac, and Jacob. Yet today, according to the United Nations and much of the Islamic world, it is considered part of the Al-Aqsa compound. But now Jewish people have begun praying in and around the Temple Mount with permission from the Israeli Knesset.

"What if," Barry asked, "an Iranian missile were to strike the mosque on the Temple Mount?"

He reminded me that an inscription on that site contains a declaration in Arabic that essentially says, "God has no son."

Then Barry asked another question he could not shake. "What if a missile from Iran were to hit the golden dome or damage the mosque in some way?"

He told me he could not get that thought out of his mind. In previous wars, missiles have already been aimed at Jerusalem. Israel has intercepted many of them, even one that came dangerously close to the Temple Mount during last year's conflict.

Barry said that if such a strike ever happened, the Islamic world might suddenly turn against Israel in a massive way. Iran could declare what it would call a holy war, rallying nations against Israel.

Even now, tensions continue to rise. Just recently, the PLO warned Israel about religious Jews attempting any sacrifices on the Temple Mount during Passover. These kinds of warnings can inflame the entire region.

Barry's point was simple: What if God is allowing events to move toward something much bigger? If something dramatic were to happen on the Temple Mount, it could become the spark that draws the nations into open confrontation with Israel.

That is why it is so important in this hour that we stay sensitive to the Holy Spirit. We need wisdom. We need discernment. We cannot believe every voice or every headline. We must measure everything by Scripture.

And I believe there has never been a more important time to respond to God. Darkness is increasing, but today is still the day of salvation. Today is the time to open our hearts to the God of Abraham, Isaac, and Jacob—and to His Messiah, Yeshua.

All of history is moving toward Jerusalem.

DECEPTION TARGETING THE CHURCH

The US Treasury Department trains its agents on what authentic money looks and feels like. After training on the authentic, the counterfeit is easy to spot! That's what I do. I train my viewers in the biblically authentic supernatural. Then, as the counterfeit increases according to Scripture, you will not be deceived.

The Bible warns that in the last days, many will fall away because they cannot discern between the real and the counterfeit. But those who know God's Word and His Glory will not be deceived!

As I write this, we are in a season I call "the Big Fix." God is giving His people the opportunity to let Him repair what is broken—our lives, our families, our health, our finances, and even the foundations we've been standing on. As believers and leaders, we need to put our own houses in order so we are prepared for what God is about to do. And at the same time, a great harvest is beginning. I believe we are about to see one of the greatest influxes of souls we've ever seen, especially among young people who are searching for something real.

This is a season of fixing what is broken before exposure makes it unavoidable. A season when hidden things are being brought into the light—not to shame but to save. A season when deception is increasing, but so is the harvest. Hunger for the authentic is exploding!

The question is not whether this is a significant moment. It is. The question is whether we will recognize it while there is still time to step through it because the window God is opening now is not only about Israel's future but about the harvest that follows and the role the church is meant to play in it.

All You Need Is Love?

I once heard a popular Christian television host say the best way to reach Jewish people is through love. I agree we should love all people, but few Jewish people come to Jesus with the "love-only" approach. Frankly, I feel as if that is a cop-out.

Millions of believers say they love Israel. They pray for Israel. They visit Israel. They give money to help Israel. But many have never once asked a Jewish person whether they know the Messiah of Israel. Let me tell you, if you say you love Israel but never share your testimony with Jewish people, you are missing God's heart.

You read in the first part of this book that I used to be a stockbroker at Merrill Lynch, and then I became a believer. And God in His sovereignty elevated me before I'd even read the New Testament, when the front page of a major newspaper in Washington, DC, printed a story about me becoming a believer in Jesus. There's one part of that story I didn't share earlier that I'll share now.

After that article appeared, I got many phone calls from people who knew me. One of them was from a woman who had been my client when I was a stockbroker. Guess what she said? "Oh, my husband and I are rejoicing. We so wanted you to become a believer."

I wanted to be gracious, so I didn't say this, but I thought, "But you never told me about Jesus. I almost lost my mind and my life until Jesus revealed Himself to me. You could have saved me a lot of grief. You wanted me saved, but you never opened your mouth."

Many Christians want their Jewish friends saved. They say, "I'll just love them." But you're not saved just by being loved by someone. You are saved through believing the gospel. You believe because you hear. If you don't hear the words of God, you won't believe.

Sharing your faith with Jewish people does not require pressure or arguments. It requires courage and compassion.

Sometimes it starts with a simple question: "I've had an experience with the Jewish Messiah—can I tell you about it?" When spoken with humility and love, that invitation opens a door.

I've included appendixes C and D to help you with this. In appendix C, I share insights I've learned over many years about how to share the gospel with Jewish people in a way they are receptive to. I believe it will be a valuable tool for you as you step into your assignment in this hour. In appendix D, I've provided Isaiah 53, which I encourage you to read to Jewish people as I did to my father.

What About Humanitarian Work?

Let me start my answer by sharing an example. Years before missiles filled the sky on October 7, 2023, God spoke to us about building bomb shelters in Israel. At the time, it made little sense. There was no urgency in the air, no headlines demanding action, no visible reason to move. I assumed God meant a single shelter—something symbolic, something modest. But God had bigger plans.

During the first seventy-two hours of the Israel-Hamas War that violently erupted on October 7, 2023, there was a fierce battle. We had strategically placed our bomb shelters in areas with the greatest need. One of our shelters was placed at Kibbutz Be'eri. This kibbutz suffered great losses of life; many were kidnapped and held hostage. Our signs were blown off in the battle and lay on the ground. In one of the attacked cities, every sign was ripped away—except the METV (Middle East TV) sign, which remained miraculously upright. Why is this so miraculous? Because our METV television network boldly proclaims the gospel 24/7 and is available on every TV in Israel, across the entire Middle East, in South Africa, and in parts of Asia!

That is not just a testimony. It is a pattern: God reveals, we believe, and we act. Today we have built three hundred bomb shelters in Israel. We work with the IDF to know where to put them. Lives are being saved. One bomb shelter weighs thirty tons, or about sixty thousand pounds. And we have three hundred of them. Only God could have done this.

I have visited congregations that are the very best in doing humanitarian work. They operate in friendship evangelism but don't share the gospel. I applaud them for their Jewish humanitarian work. But what good is feeding a Jewish person with food and intentionally withholding the gospel?

Humanitarian work is good and necessary, but it must be paired with the message of Messiah. Paul said it clearly in Romans 10:14: "How then shall they call on Him in whom they have not believed? And how shall they believe in Him of whom they have not heard? And how shall they hear without a preacher?"

Food, shelter, and medicine matter, but if we meet every physical need and never share the truth about Yeshua, we have not loved people fully.

Let me put it another way. If Jewish people receive humanitarian aid without the gospel, many of them could spend eternity separated from God. What was meant to help them could result in a massive number of Jewish people's final exit being hell! That is not love. Real love brings help along with the good news of the Messiah.

So you must ask yourself a simple question: Am I funding projects that only comfort people temporarily, or am I supporting work that also introduces them to the Messiah who gives eternal life?

This is why we have committed our ministry to practical, scalable ways to reach Jewish people. We consider it our mission to pioneer historic Jewish evangelism. Just look at what God has done through our ministry in recent years.

We have conducted outreaches called "Lectures on the Supernatural" in which mostly Jewish people have made public professions of faith; a majority of them were in the land of Israel.

We have mailed or distributed copies of my Jewish evangelistic testimony books to Jewish families.

Our web page offers a free download of my Jewish testimony book from viewing my one-minute Jewish evangelistic ads on Fox News, Fox Business, Newsmax, MSNBC, and CNBC.

We have a one-hour supernatural, evangelistic television special on the first Sunday of every month on Newsmax.

We broadcast our evangelistic television network—Middle East Television (METV)—to every cable and satellite subscriber in Israel, as well as the entire Middle East, 24/7 at no charge.

We sow the seed of the Word and cover it with prayer, trusting God to bring the increase. You may never meet the person who reads something you helped to send, but heaven will record the fruit.

This is Genesis 12:3 with a name and a mailbox. When you go to the Jew first, you open a door of blessing. In this scripture, God promises to bless those who bless the Jewish people. What is the greatest way to bless the Jewish people? Tell them about the good news of Jesus. When you do this, you are planting a seed that will result in a harvest of both Jewish and Gentile souls.

When the Harvest Is Complete

Everything God is doing right now is moving toward the finish line. The increase of His Glory, the harvest of souls, and the return to God's order are not separate things. They are all part of the same story God has been writing from the beginning. And God always finishes what He starts.

The return of the Messiah is not an interruption of history. It is the fulfillment of it. We often speak of His return as a future event, but the truth is, it could happen before you even finish this book! However, Scripture makes it clear that an end-time harvest comes before Jesus returns. And before the harvest, God prepares His people.

This is why the gospel must return to where it began. The good news started in Israel and spread to the nations, and it will return to the Jewish people—not to repeat the story but to complete it. And when the Jewish people recognize their Messiah, the Bible tells us it will be like life from the dead, not only for Israel but for the whole world.

This is the final harvest we are moving toward.

This is what the Glory has been preparing us for. God is not asking us to predict dates or figure out timelines. He is asking us to be ready.

Ready to walk in truth.

Ready to carry His Presence.

Ready to participate in the harvest.

Ready to stand with Israel—not only in words but in witness.

The greatest mistake the church could make in this hour is to admire what God is doing but never step into it. The greatest privilege is to recognize the moment and say yes to Him.

Because the story is coming full circle. What God promised will happen. What has been planted in faith will be gathered in Glory.

And the Messiah is returning—not for a passive people but for a prepared people. So may we be found faithful as God finishes the harvest and brings His story to its appointed end.

And the question that remains is simple: Will we be ready when He comes?

Conclusion

WHEN THE GLORY FILLS THE EARTH

RECENTLY, I INTERVIEWED a prophet who shared a word that confirmed what others have spoken over me across many years. She said I was called to carry light just before widespread darkness. That the global rise of deception and anti-Semitism is not accidental but the very environment I was born to confront with demonstrations of God's supernatural power.

She spoke of voices calling the remnant by name. Of testimony awakening nations. Of aged wine poured last and poured strong. She said the Jewish harvest is not coming, but it has already begun, and I will be one of its trumpets. She said the next generation of Messianic Jewish prophets is watching what we're doing.

I do not share this to elevate myself. I share it to testify to God's faithfulness and to declare this: That word was not just for me. It was for you too.

God is not interested in reproducing yesterday's moves. He is writing something fresh—handwritten by Him.

So where is Messianic Vision headed? I'll make it as plain as possible: God is going to reach more Jewish people through Messianic Vision than any ministry in history. And when the gospel goes to the Jew first, it will reach more

Gentiles than by any other means. This is not strategy. It is God's order.

Jewish people are scattered across the earth. You cannot reach Israel without touching the nations. And you cannot participate in the completed harvest without honoring what God established at the beginning.

The Question That Matters Most

As the Glory increases, the questions get simpler—and more serious. The most important question I have right now is not about the future of nations or the direction of the church. It is personal.

Do you have a healthy fear of God? Have you repented of every known sin?

If I could give you one instruction—doctor's orders, if you will—it would be this: Live in instant repentance. Repent quickly. Repent honestly. Repent while your heart is still tender. Sin tolerated over time hardens your heart. Sin confessed immediately loses its grip.

Without the fear of the Lord, the Glory has no safe place to land in your life. Signs and wonders will increase—but Scripture also warns that false signs and wonders will increase. Only a repentant, yielded heart will discern the difference. Only a life submitted to God can carry His Presence without distortion.

How Then Should You Live?

What you have read in this book is true. Neutrality is no longer an option for you. These days require intentional living. You are being called to

- live in ongoing repentance, not occasional correction;
- refuse compromise, even when it is culturally celebrated;
- speak with boldness and humility, rooted in love and truth;
- stand with God's covenant purposes, especially concerning Israel; and
- depend daily on the Holy Spirit, not yesterday's encounters.

The Greater Glory does not need spectators. It needs carriers. God is not asking you for perfection. He is asking for availability. Not polish but purity of heart. Not noise but obedience.

A MOMENT OF DECISION

You are living in days when many, even Christians, are turning away from Israel. God is watching. Not with anger but with searching eyes.

He is looking for people like you, men and women who will stand with His covenant purposes. Who will speak when silence is easier. Who will choose clarity over convenience.

These are not easy days, but they are glorious ones. God told us there would be both apostasy and outpouring, confusion and clarity, pressure and Presence. But He also promised that His Glory will be there.

The question is whether you will be.

THE RELATIONSHIP THAT CHANGES EVERYTHING

What God is ultimately inviting you into is not a movement, a ministry, or even a moment. It is a relationship. A relationship with the God of Abraham, Isaac, and Jacob. And yes, whether you expect it or not, that relationship centers on Jesus.

Messiah is not a Gentile idea imposed on Jewish faith. He is the fulfillment of covenant. The One Israel has been waiting for. The One the nations were promised.

When Jewish people recognize Messiah, resurrection life follows—not just individually but corporately. Life from the dead. A restored people releasing restored purpose.

God is not looking for perfect people. He is looking for yielded people. People who stay tender. People who repent quickly. People who love truth enough to obey it. And people who will not be ashamed of Jesus—Yeshua—when it is easier to stay quiet.

Let this book do what it was meant to do: bring you closer to Him.

NOW IT'S YOUR TURN

Many believe they are basically "good" because they have a "good" heart. God says differently: "The heart is more deceitful than all things and desperately wicked" (Jer. 17:9).

But God loved you too much to leave you in that condition. And you know how much love God has for those who love Him—even for those who don't love Him? Jeremiah 31:3 (NKJV) says, "The LORD has appeared of old to me, saying: Yes, I have loved you with an everlasting love; therefore with lovingkindness I have drawn you."

Everlasting love. How long? Everlasting. He is pure love. He cannot help but love you.

This is why He says through His Jewish prophet Ezekiel,

> Then I will sprinkle clean water on you, and you shall be clean. I will cleanse you from all your filthiness and from all your idols. I will give you a new heart and put a new spirit within you; I will take the heart of stone out of your flesh and give you a heart of flesh.
>
> —Ezekiel 36:25–26, nkjv

The Messiah came to earth the first time to suffer and pay the penalty for your sins so you could be clean and receive a new heart. He will come a second time to usher in an age of peace on earth. How could there ever be peace on earth with wicked hearts?

I have personally experienced the promise you are about to read from the Bible in my own life. I know this will also be true for you. How do I know this? God loves you as much as He loves me.

The Bible promises in Romans 10:9, 13 (nkjv): "If you confess with your mouth the Lord Jesus and believe in your heart that God has raised Him from the dead, you will be saved.…'Whoever calls on the name of the Lord shall be saved.'"

God has taken the first step. Now it is your turn. We all need a supernatural heart transplant. God wants to give you a new heart filled with His love and to place His Spirit inside you. Some, like me, will have a dramatic encounter when they receive a new heart. Others will accept this forgiveness by faith.

You may or may not feel anything. My wife, Joy, felt nothing when she first prayed to God for a new heart. But as time went by, she realized she had changed and that God was living inside her. Not everyone has a dramatic testimony like mine. Joy's is more the norm.

Your first step is based on a decision. The feelings and experiences will come as you grow in knowing God by reading the Bible. That's the main reason why it is important to read the Bible. I would start with the New Testament. This will cause you to grow rapidly in the knowledge of the Messiah.

To know God is everything. To have everything and not know God is nothing. If you do not know God before you die, you will not know Him after you die.

Now say this prayer out loud and believe it to the best of your ability:

> *Dear God, I confess that I have sinned against You, and I am truly sorry for it. Messiah Yeshua, please come into my heart and life and cleanse me with Your precious blood of atonement. Give me a new heart filled with Your love. In Yeshua's name, amen.*

Welcome into the *Mishpochah* (family) of God!

Your Part in the Story

God's Presence, power, and activity in the world are not weakening as history moves forward. Even when it looks like faith is declining or darkness is growing, God is intensifying His work. What God is doing now is greater, not lesser, than what He has done before.

God is not losing ground. The darkness is not winning. Israel is being restored, the church is being completed, and the Messiah will be revealed. What's happening now is not the end of everything or a collapse into chaos. Instead, it is the moment when all of God's purposes throughout history—His covenant with Israel, the role of the church, the revelation of Messiah, and the outpouring of His Spirit—are coming back into their proper order and position.

Everything God has been doing has been moving toward this moment: Jew and Gentile, one in Messiah, carrying the same Presence and fulfilling the same purpose.

But before I close this book, I want to take you back to where the story really began—on a road.

Years ago, I was on another road at a completely different place in my life. I didn't know God. I wasn't looking for Him. In fact, I wanted to disappear. But God intervened.

That moment became the beginning of everything. If God had not stepped in on that road, I never would have come to know my Messiah. This testimony would never have been spoken. The witness that has gone out through this ministry would never have gone out. The voice that has reached millions of people around the world would never have been released.

That was the first time God preserved my life for a purpose. Years later, I found myself on another road. This time, I knew God. This time, I was walking in the calling He had given me. But suddenly, I hit ice on an exit ramp in

Charlotte. The car spun. I had no control. I could not steer. I could not stop.

In a moment, everything could have ended. But once again, God intervened.

Two young men appeared at exactly the right moment. They pulled my car free, got me back on the road, and then disappeared as quickly as they came. I never got their names. I don't know where they came from or where they went. But I know this. They were there on assignment.

Two roads. Two moments. Two times my life could have ended. But both times, God stepped in.

The first time, He preserved my life so the testimony could begin. The second time, He preserved my life so the testimony would not be silenced.

Do you see it? This was never just about survival. It was about a witness, about a voice, and about a testimony that had to go out.

The Bible speaks about the seal of testimony—a witness that God establishes so that His truth can be carried into the earth. And that testimony is not meant to stay with one person. It becomes a witness that spreads and awakens a remnant: men and women who hear the voice of God, who carry His Presence, and who are sent out to declare what He has done.

That is what this book has been about: God raising up a people who will carry His Glory. A remnant who will go out with the witness of Messiah to the nations—and especially to the Jewish people. Because the awakening of Israel is not the end of the story. It is the catalyst for the greatest harvest the world has ever seen.

And now the invitation is in front of you. God is not just preserving a message. He is raising up messengers. People who will carry His Presence. People who will walk in His Glory. People who will become part of the remnant He is sending into the earth.

I have often tried to imagine what this earth would look like if it were saturated with the Greater Glory. I believe entire families will be restored. I believe entire blocks of homes will be filled with God's Glory. Yes, even entire states and countries will be known for the Glory.

At the same time, the devil will be doing the same thing with his power. But I have read the end of the Bible: "Look, I am coming soon! My reward is with Me to give to each one according to his work" (Rev. 22:12).

The choice is completely yours. "The Spirit and the bride say, 'Come.' Let anyone who is thirsty come" (v. 17, NLT, emphasis added).

Light always triumphs over darkness!

This is the Glory Story. And it is not just my story. It is yours. The best is not behind you. The best is yet to come.

Appendix A

ISRAEL, MY GLORY: A GUIDE TO ISRAEL'S ROLE IN GOD'S PLAN

When Scripture speaks of Israel, it does so with a gravity unlike any other nation. Israel is not just part of biblical history; she is woven into the structure of redemption itself. To understand Israel is not simply to understand a people, but to understand how God reveals His faithfulness, His covenant, and His Glory in the earth.

The Bible says Israel was created for end-time Glory.

Isaiah 43:6–7 says, "Bring My sons from afar and My daughters from the ends of the earth, even everyone who is called by My name, for I have created him for My glory; I have formed him, and I have made him."

Why was Israel created? For God's Glory.

Isaiah 46:13 (NKJV) also says, "I will place salvation in Zion, for Israel My glory." Glory for whom? Israel. That phrase, "Israel My glory," is not sentimental language. It reflects a biblical reality: God has chosen to make His character, purposes, and redemptive intent visible through a specific people, in a specific land, across time. Israel exists not because history preserved her but because God did.

Covenant, Not Replacement

From Genesis to Revelation, Scripture presents God's covenant with Israel as enduring and irrevocable. The calling of Abraham was not provisional. It was not symbolic. It was covenantal. God bound His promises to Abraham's descendants with His own name and reputation.

The apostle Paul addresses this directly when he insists that God has not rejected His people and that the gifts and calling of God are irrevocable. This is foundational. Any understanding of redemption that requires God to abandon Israel misunderstands both covenant and character.

Belief in Messiah does not erase Jewish identity. It fulfills it. The New Covenant does not cancel the Old; it reveals what was always contained within it. Israel remains Israel—not as an obstacle to redemption, but as its original vessel.

Glory and Election

Throughout Scripture the Glory of God is repeatedly associated with Israel. God's Presence descended among them in the wilderness. His Glory filled the tabernacle and later the Temple. His name was placed upon them, not because of merit but because of purpose.

Glory, in biblical terms, is not emotional atmosphere. It is the manifest Presence of God—revealed, weighty, authoritative. Israel's calling has always been connected to making that Glory known.

Paul makes a striking statement in Romans 9:4 when he lists Israel's unique privileges and declares that the Glory belongs to them. Israel's role in history is inseparable from God's desire to reveal Himself.

Israel and the Nations

God's election of Israel was never meant to exclude the nations. From the beginning, Israel was chosen for the sake of the world. The promise to Abraham made this explicit: Through his descendants all the families of the earth would be blessed.

This establishes a pattern that Scripture never abandons. Blessing flows outward from Israel to the nations. Redemption moves through Israel before it reaches the ends of the earth. This is not favoritism; it is divine order.

The nations are not redeemed apart from Israel, nor is Israel redeemed apart from Messiah. Jew and Gentile are brought together in Him—not by erasing distinction but by fulfilling purpose.

Blessing and Consequence

Scripture consistently links blessing and consequence to how individuals and nations respond to God's covenant with Israel. This principle is not political, nor is it cultural. It is spiritual.

God's promise to bless those who bless Israel and oppose those who oppose her (Gen. 12:3) is not a slogan—it is a covenant reality that unfolds across history. The Bible presents Israel as a measuring rod that reveals where we stand. We're not siding with a nation but with God's purposes.

This does not mean Israel is beyond accountability or correction. Scripture is clear that God disciplines those He loves (Heb. 12:6). But discipline is not rejection. Correction is not cancellation. Israel's continued existence testifies to God's faithfulness, not Israel's perfection.

Restoration, Not Elevation

To affirm Israel's role is not to elevate her above the nations but to recognize God's design. Israel's restoration is not about dominance; it is about fulfillment. Scripture points toward a future where Israel recognizes her Messiah and fulfills her calling as a light to the nations. (See Isaiah 60:3.)

This restoration does not diminish the church. It completes her.

When Israel and the church stand together in Messiah, God's redemptive plan comes into full view. What began with covenant reaches culmination in unity.

Israel in the Purposes of God

Throughout history the Jewish people lived in fear and persecution in nation after nation. We were scattered to the four corners of the earth. Yet we were preserved as a distinct people against impossible odds. This is not an accident of history. It is evidence of purpose. Empires have risen and fallen. Cultures have disappeared. Israel remains.

And God said He would regather us. Isaiah 11:12 (NKJV) says, "He will set up a banner for the nations and will assemble the outcasts of Israel, and gather together the dispersed of Judah from the four corners of the earth."

Israel's story is unfinished. Scripture points toward a future awakening, a restoration that brings life from the dead—not only for Israel but for the world. This awakening is not separate from the gospel. It is the gospel reaching its intended fullness.

God has a strategy. His strategy has always been to go to the Jew first. That is exactly what happened in the early church. Twelve Jewish apostles turned the world upside down.

But what if this time God begins with a thousand Jewish believers instead of twelve? Or ten thousand? Or a hundred thousand?

Do you see what I'm saying? I believe the Glory of God is going to rest on Israel. And when it does, the Jewish people will carry that Glory to the nations. The Bible talks about 144,000 end-time evangelists. But I believe it will be far more than that. And I believe millions of Gentiles will come to the Lord.

Because the Bible says, "Salvation is of the Jews" (John 4:22).

A Covenant That Reveals Glory

To say, "Israel, My Glory," is to affirm that God reveals Himself through covenant faithfulness. Israel's role in redemptive history declares that God keeps His promises across generations, even when circumstances seem to contradict them.

God's Glory does not bypass Israel. It passes through her—just as it always has.

Understanding this truth anchors your spiritual beliefs. It clarifies prophecy and restores your connection to God's heart. It also reminds you that God's plans are not reactive, fragmented, or abandoned. They are purposeful, continuous, and sure.

Israel remains central—not as a spiritual obstacle but as a living testimony that God's Word stands forever.

Appendix B

KEY SCRIPTURES ON ISRAEL AND THE GLORY

I HAVE LEARNED OVER the years that the safest place to stand is on Scripture. Here are a few of my favorite Scriptures on Israel and the Glory.

Light/Glory Dispels All Darkness

Genesis 1:1–4

> In the beginning God created the heavens and the earth. The earth was formless and void [containing nothing], darkness was over the surface of the deep, and the Spirit of God was moving over the surface of the water. God said, "Let there be light [Glory]," and there was light [Glory]. God saw that the light was good, and God separated the light from the darkness.

What Is the Glory?

Exodus 33:18–19

> Then Moses said, "I pray, show me Your glory."
>
> Then He said, "I will make all My goodness pass before you." [Glory is the goodness or love that pours out of and surrounds God.]

Too Thick to Enter

Exodus 40:34–35

> Then the cloud covered the tent of meeting, and the glory of the Lord filled the tabernacle. Moses was not able to enter into the tent of meeting because the cloud settled on it, and the glory of the Lord filled the tabernacle.

Couldn't Stand in the Glory

2 Chronicles 5:13–14

> It happened, when the trumpet players and singers made one sound to praise and give thanks to the Lord, and when they lifted up their voice with the trumpets and cymbals and all the instruments of music and praised the Lord saying, "For He is good and His mercy endures forever," that the house, the house of the Lord, was filled with a cloud. And the priests were not able to stand in order to serve because of the cloud, for the glory of the Lord had filled the house of God.

Near Future

John 14:12

> He who believes in Me will do the [same] works that I do also. And he will do greater works than these [because of the Greater Glory].

Haggai 2:9

The glory of this latter house will be greater than the former, says the LORD of Hosts. And in this place I will give peace [shalom], says the LORD of Hosts.

Habakkuk 2:14

For the earth will be filled with the knowledge of the glory of the LORD.

Psalm 91:1

He who dwells [exists] in the shelter [secret place] of the Most High shall abide under the shadow [glory] of the Almighty.

Fire in the Glory

2 Chronicles 7:1

And when Solomon finished praying, fire came down from the heavens and consumed the burnt offering and sacrifices, and the glory of the LORD filled the temple.

Glory Can Be Seen

Isaiah 60:1–3

Arise, shine, for your light has come, and the glory of the LORD has risen upon you. For the darkness shall cover the earth and deep darkness the peoples; but the LORD shall rise upon you, and His glory shall be seen upon you. The nations shall come to your light and kings to the brightness of your rising.

God's Light in the Glory

Revelation 21:23

> The city has no need of sun or moon to shine in it, for the glory of God is its light, and its lamp is the Lamb.

Appendix C

HOW TO SHARE JESUS WITH JEWISH PEOPLE

I AM OFTEN ASKED how to communicate the good news with Jewish people. What follows is not a formula but a biblical framework I have used for decades.

1. Begin with expectancy

Sharing Messiah is not a technique—it is a Spirit-led encounter. I never rely on persuasion alone. I rely on the Holy Spirit, who reveals truth and confirms it with His Presence.

My direction from God is easy and biblical. In 1 Corinthians 1:22, Paul says, "For the Jews require a sign." I ask whether the Jewish person or any person has any pain. I then pray, and the pain leaves. Then I have earned the right to present the gospel.

If you do not move in signs and wonders, I have advice for you that worked for me: Always look for someone sick or in pain or on crutches and pray for them. Keep praying for people even if you don't see healings or miracles. Don't give up.

In God's time, you will walk in signs and wonders, but believe everyone you pray for is instantly healed before you see it. If not immediately, tell them to keep believing.

You are not moved by results. You are moved by the Word of God. Through faith and patience on your part and on the part of the person you pray for, you will inherit the promises! (See Hebrews 6:12.)

Key truth: God reveals Himself; we bear witness.

Key Scriptures: Zechariah 4:6; John 16:13; Acts 1:8

2. What it means to be a "true Jew"

The word *Jew* comes from a Hebrew root meaning praiser of God. That raises an important question: How can someone truly praise God if they do not know Him personally?

Key truth: Knowing about God is not the same as knowing God.

Key Scriptures: Jeremiah 31:33–34; Daniel 12:2; John 17:3

3. Start with the Hebrew Scriptures

When speaking with Jewish people, I begin with the Tanakh. It is our shared authority and common ground. I do not argue theology; I open Scripture.

Key truth: God speaks for Himself through His Word.

Key Scriptures: Isaiah 8:20; Luke 24:27; Acts 17:2–3

4. God's credibility revealed through Jewish history

The Bible makes precise predictions about the Jewish people—our blessing, judgment, scattering, preservation, and regathering. History itself testifies that God's Word is true.

Key truths: Israel's dispersion and persecution were foretold, Jewish preservation defies natural explanation, and regathering to the land is a public sign to the nations.

Key Scriptures: Deuteronomy 28; Isaiah 11:12; Isaiah 66:8; Jeremiah 31:35–36

5. The necessity of blood atonement

The Torah is explicit: Atonement requires blood. The sacrificial system was never an end—it was a shadow pointing toward God's ultimate provision.

Key truth: Without blood atonement, biblical forgiveness does not exist.

Key Scriptures: Leviticus 17:11; Exodus 12:7, 13; Isaiah 53:5–6

6. The promise of the New Covenant

The New Covenant is not about adopting a new religion. It is about knowing God personally. God writes His law on the heart and removes sin completely—not just covering it.

Key truths: God internalizes His Torah, relationship replaces ritual, and sin is forgiven and remembered no more.

Key Scriptures: Jeremiah 31:31–34; Ezekiel 36:26–27

7. One Messiah, two appearances

The Hebrew Scriptures describe a Messiah who suffers and a Messiah who reigns. I believe they point to one Messiah with two comings—first to atone, later to rule.

Key truth: God sent one Messiah, not many.

Key Scriptures: Isaiah 53; Psalm 22; Zechariah 12:10; Isaiah 9:6–7

8. Key Messianic prophecies

There are hundreds of prophetic markers about Messiah. I usually focus on Isaiah 53, which is why I provide a copy of it in appendix D.

Key Scriptures: Micah 5:2 (birthplace); Isaiah 7:14 (sign of Messiah); Isaiah 11:1, 10 (Davidic line and Gentile hope); Zechariah 11:12–13 (betrayal price); Daniel 9:25–26 (Messiah before temple destruction)

9. Communicate with wisdom and sensitivity

Jewish people carry deep historical wounds connected to Christian language and imagery. I never change the message—but I remove unnecessary obstacles.

Practical guidance: Use Messiah rather than Christ when possible. The word *Christ* comes from the Greek, but the word *Messiah* comes from the Hebrew. Also, avoid words like crusade or convert. For example, the word *convert* has a negative connotation because of being forced to convert or die. Speak of "the Jewish people," not "the Jew." Be mindful of imagery that may hinder conversation.

Key Scriptures: 1 Corinthians 9:19–23; Colossians 4:5–6; Romans 14:13

10. Explaining God's triune nature

As a Jew shaped by the Sh'ma, I emphasize God's triune nature revealed in Scripture. God is one—yet He reveals Himself as Father, Messiah, and Spirit.

Key truth: God is one in essence, revealed in fullness.

Key Scriptures: Deuteronomy 6:4; Isaiah 59:20–21; Isaiah 7:14; Genesis 1:2

11. Repentance: turning fully to God

Repentance is not regret—it is a decisive turn. We turn away from sin and continue turning toward God for the power to change.

Key truths: God's standard is holiness, repentance is active and ongoing, and Messiah empowers transformation.

Key Scriptures: Ezekiel 18:30–32; Isaiah 55:6–7; Psalm 51:1–4

12. The eternal choice

Scripture presents a sober reality: everlasting life or everlasting separation. Love does not hide that truth—it speaks it clearly and compassionately.

Key Scriptures: Daniel 12:2; Jeremiah 31:34

13. Pray for the peace of Jerusalem

Scripture commands us to pray for Jerusalem's *shalom*—completeness. True peace flows from knowing the God of Abraham, Isaac, and Jacob.

Key Scripture: Psalm 122:6

Suggested Prayer

God of Abraham, Isaac, and Jacob, I have sinned against You. I turn away from my sin and turn toward You. I believe You have provided atonement through the Messiah. I ask You to forgive me, cleanse me, and write Your truth on my heart. I want to know You—not just know about You. Live inside me. Lead me in Your ways and fill me with Your Spirit. Amen.

Appendix D

ISAIAH 53

Who has believed our report? And to whom has the arm of the LORD been revealed? For he grew up before Him as a tender plant and as a root out of a dry ground. He has no form or majesty that we should look upon him nor appearance that we should desire him. He was despised and rejected of men, a man of sorrows and acquainted with grief. And we hid, as it were, our faces from him; he was despised, and we did not esteem him.

Surely he has borne our grief and carried our sorrows; Yet we esteemed him stricken, smitten of God, and afflicted. But he was wounded for our transgressions, he was bruised for our iniquities; the chastisement of our peace was upon him, and by his stripes we are healed. All of us like sheep have gone astray; each of us has turned to his own way, but the LORD has laid on him the iniquity of us all.

He was oppressed, and he was afflicted, yet he opened not his mouth; he was brought as a lamb to the slaughter, and as a sheep before its shearers is silent, so he opened not his mouth. By oppression and judgment he was taken away, and who shall declare his generation? For he was cut off out of the land of the living; for the transgression of my people he was struck. His grave was assigned with the wicked, yet with the rich in his death, because he had done no violence, nor was any deceit in his mouth.

Yet it pleased the LORD to bruise him; He has put him to grief. If he made himself as an offering for sin, he shall see his offspring, he shall prolong his days, and the good pleasure of the LORD shall prosper in his hand. He shall see of the anguish of his soul and be satisfied. By his knowledge My righteous servant shall justify the many, for he shall bear their iniquities. Therefore, I will divide him a portion with the great, and he shall divide the spoil with the strong, because he poured out his soul to death, and he was numbered with the transgressors, thus he bore the sin of many and made intercession for the transgressors.

THE GLORY STORY IN PICTURES

ACT 1—THE MAKING OF A BELIEVER

Sid Roth with his father, who was born in Poland and narrowly escaped the Holocaust. For decades, he resisted Sid's faith in Yeshua but ultimately accepted Jesus as Messiah on his deathbed at age eighty-three.

Sid as a young boy (left) and at his bar mitzvah at age thirteen (right): Raised in an Orthodox Jewish family, Sid was shaped early by tradition—and by Perthes hip disease, a childhood challenge that strengthened his determination to overcome the limitations others placed on him.

A portrait of Sid in the 1970s, shortly after becoming one of the earliest public Jewish believers in Jesus of his generation.

WASHINGTON'S NEW EVANGELISTS

White collar 'Jesus Freaks'

By JERRY OPPENHEIMER

Copyright 1972 by The Washington Daily News

"IF Jesus goes, 'Boo,' I jump," declares Sid Roth, 31-year-old, $30,000-a-year vice president of a prosperous Arlington brokerage house. "If Jesus says go to Africa, I take off. But I believe Jesus wants me in the investment business. I don't question my God."

Up until a few months ago, Sid Roth was an aggressive, hard-nosed businessman, and an orthodox Jew. Today, gazing out of the expansive picture window in his starkly modern sixth-floor suite, Sid Roth says, "I had been searching for something all my life. I never found anything I really dug. I didn't know what I was searching for — until I found Jesus."

Then Sid Roth leans forward in his deep leather chair, proudly points to a little gold pin with the letters "PTL" on his stylishly wide lapel and whispers, "Ask me what it means, come on, ask me what it means."

What does it mean?

has surfaced in the establishment business world. White collar Jesus Freaks. They tote [illegible]

[illegible] "Baptism of the Holy Spirit," and during a series of interviews with a number of white collar Jesus Freaks in their offices, they were most eager to demonstrate this new-found power with a little "miracle" known in the movement as

On February 29, 1972, *The Washington Daily News* ran a front-page story about a group it called the "White Collar Jesus Freaks," and Sid was among them. Though he had asked the Jewish reporter to keep his comments off the record, nearly everything he said appeared in print. The article caught the attention of healing evangelist Kathryn Kuhlman.

Sid with healing evangelist Kathryn Kuhlman on her television program, *I Believe in Miracles*. Kuhlman's ministry was marked by healing and a deep reverence for the presence of God. After the interview, she offered to mentor Sid if he would relocate to Pittsburgh. He declined—not yet understanding how rare her ministry was. It is a decision, he writes, that has followed him ever since.

Sid preaching at a Messianic congregation in the early years of his ministry: At a time when Jewish believers in Yeshua were exceptionally rare, Sid helped pioneer the modern Messianic movement, which spread to major cities across the United States and around the world.

Sid speaking at Beth Messiah Congregation in Rockville, Maryland, one of the pioneering Messianic congregations in America. The congregation began with about fifteen core members who met in an apartment, then grew into one of the premier Messianic congregations in the United States and a model for Jewish evangelism.

Sid with his wife, Joy, and daughter Leigh at Beth Messiah Congregation: Joy came to faith not through argument but through watching Sid's changed life over many months. Leigh came to the Lord at a weekend Christian retreat. Sid writes that seeing his family come to Yeshua blessed him beyond measure.

ACT 2–THE VISION

Sid signing one of the early ministry agreements that helped expand Messianic outreach during a time when public Jewish witness for Yeshua was still rare.

Much of Sid's ministry began not on a stage but behind a desk—praying, studying Scripture, and seeking God's direction for the next assignment.

An early promotional photograph of Sid at the microphone. He was initially recruited as an announcer by Messianic Jewish leader Manny Brotman but resisted the role, preferring to work behind the scenes. But he soon discovered he had a gift for radio ministry. His Washington, DC, radio show became the top Jewish radio program on Sunday mornings in that market. He deliberately purchased the time slot immediately following a popular traditional Jewish program, so that its audience flowed directly into his.

Behind the microphone at WMCA Radio in New York, Sid Roth discovered a powerful way to share the reality of the Messiah with thousands of listeners. What began as a radio broadcast became a platform for testimonies, miracles, and the supernatural power of God to reach people around the world. Those early days on the air helped lay the foundation for a ministry that would impact millions.

Sid during an early radio interview in Brunswick, Georgia. Radio became one of his earliest and most effective tools for reaching Jewish people with the gospel.

Sid is shown hosting his live call-in show in New York City, where he openly made the case each week that Jesus was the Jewish Messiah. He describes the weekly trip to New York as invading the enemy's territory.

Sid was instructed in a dream to find and interview Jewish people who had broken through the mold of their previous experiences to achieve their destiny. *They Thought for Themselves* grew out of Sid's conviction that Jewish testimonies are one of the most effective tools for reaching Jewish people.

THE MESSIANIC VISION

P.O. BOX 34444 WASHINGTON D.C. 20034

APRIL 1977 VOLUME 1 — NO. 1

THE CALL...

by SID ROTH

Producer and Host
Messianic Vision Radio Program

I KNOW HOW ABRAHAM MUST HAVE FELT when he was called out of his comfortable home into a new, unknown land! He had ***the call*** by God. He said, "Hineni" (Here am I). Imagine having the faith to be called Abraham (father of a multitude)! Without children, at age one hundred, that takes real "chutzpah (nerve)." This is a classic example of calling those things that are not as if they are . . . the GOD KIND OF FAITH.

I ALSO RECEIVED A SOVEREIGN CALL to leave the ministry I was with for four years! God said to leave as you came in . . . take nothing with you. My former radio ministry was doing fantastically. Support was pouring in and stations were being added rapidly. To the natural mind it was foolish, but no more foolish than perhaps Abraham's call appeared. The choice was easy because God had proved to me ***I could trust Him as my source in all things.***

FOUR YEARS AGO, STARTING WITH NOTHING, He put me into the oil business. Today, I derive my income from oil investments. This enables me to devote 100% of my time in the ministry ***without drawing a salary.*** This allows more of your tithe dollars to go directly into the ministry rather than into "overhead." We're more interested in getting the message out than expensive offices or high salaries.

The inaugural issue of the Messianic Vision newsletter, April 1977, published from Washington, DC. In it, Sid explains that he derived his income from oil investments so he could devote all his time to ministry without drawing a salary, allowing every donated dollar to go directly to spreading the gospel.

Act 3—Outreach and Harvest

Sid with Orthodox rabbis in Brooklyn during the early years of his ministry. Throughout his ministry, he has sought dialogue with Jewish leaders while remaining unapologetic about his faith in Yeshua.

A Brighton Beach rabbi confronts Sid's outreach efforts among Russian Jews. Many ministries had attempted to reach the Russian Jewish community in Brighton Beach, Sid writes, and the opposition had knocked every one of them out.

Police intervened after Orthodox Jewish opponents attempted to block access to Sid's Russian Jewish outreach meeting in Brighton Beach. Every church, movie theater, and school in the neighborhood had turned Sid down when he sought a meeting space. The Board of Education finally said yes, and in the first week of Bible studies, all twenty-three people who attended came to the Lord.

Sid with Orthodox rabbis on the streets of Brighton Beach: A Russian Jewish believer who lived in the neighborhood invited Sid to share his testimony in her apartment. When he arrived, the place was packed beyond capacity. He shared the gospel, and every single person present received the Lord—something he had never seen happen before.

A crowd gathered outside a Brighton Beach meeting in Brooklyn, where approximately one hundred thousand Russian Jews lived within a ten-block radius. At one gathering, Orthodox Jews organized a blockade to prevent attendees from entering, and police had to intervene. Sid writes that while many would have wanted no part of such a confrontation, he loved it.

Sid in Moscow during one of his early ministry trips to the former Soviet Union, which initially started with Jonathan Bernis. Bernis had simply knocked on Sid's door one day, and the two became fast friends. What began as a scouting trip opened the door to a remarkable harvest among Russian Jews.

One of the venues used for Jonathan Bernis's Jewish music festivals in the former Soviet Union, where thousands of Russian Jews heard the gospel and many received Yeshua as Messiah. At Sid's first such event, he watched as people ran forward to receive the Messiah.

One of Sid's meetings in the former Soviet Union. The spiritual hunger he encountered there was unlike anything he had experienced. The anointing at those services was so powerful, he writes, that he felt people would have come forward to receive the Lord no matter what he said.

A worship gathering in the former Soviet Union. Sid writes that he did not realize at the time that he and others were making spiritual history.

Sid at the Odessa Orphanage in Ukraine. Ministry among the children became an important expression of Messianic Vision's commitment to practical compassion alongside evangelism. Today, Messianic Vision still supports evangelistic outreach and ministry in Ukraine.

During visits to Ukraine, Sid combined practical compassion with proclamation of the gospel.

Act 4—National Impact

Sid with Oprah Winfrey on *People Are Talking*, a Baltimore talk show, when both were early in their careers. Oprah challenged him, insisting a Jewish person could not believe in Jesus. Sid thought the interview was a disaster. But a Jewish woman watching at home had prayed that God would show her just one Jewish person who believed in Yeshua—and after seeing *People Are Talking* that night, she became a believer.

As the ministry continued to grow, national television became a powerful platform for proclaiming that Jesus is the Jewish Messiah.

Over the years, Sid Roth appeared frequently on *The 700 Club* and other national broadcasts, using every opportunity to point viewers to Yeshua.

Pat Boone interviews Sid Roth on TBN as Sid shares his passion for the supernatural, the Jewish people, and the saving power of Yeshua.

Whether speaking to small groups or large crowds, Sid's message has remained the same: God is real, God is supernatural, and Yeshua is the Jewish Messiah.

ACT 5—THE SUPERNATURAL MANDATE

One of the early Messianic Vision conferences that helped establish a growing national outreach.

Sharing the message of Messiah in Israel, the nation that has remained at the center of Sid's calling for more than fifty years. Throughout his ministry, sharing information about God was never enough for Sid—he wanted people to encounter the same presence that had transformed him. Everywhere he went, he shared the gospel and prayed for salvation and healing.

Praying for the sick and ministering the Presence of God has remained central to Sid's ministry from the beginning.

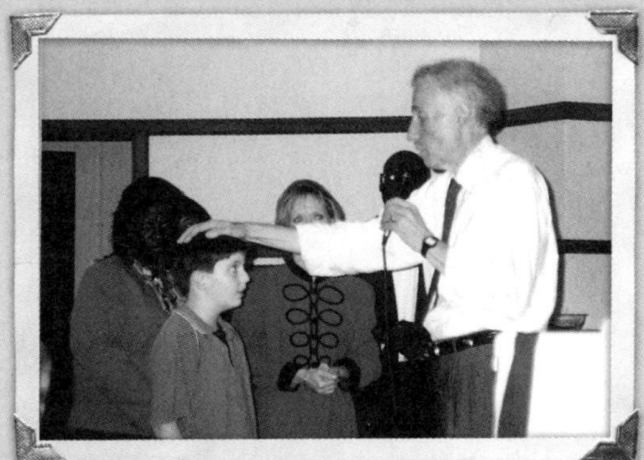

Sid ministering at an outreach. He writes that God showed up every time he prayed—and that the experience of the miraculous was never optional for him but was central to reaching Jewish people, since the Jewish heart, he believes, is uniquely opened by authentic demonstrations of God's power.

In 1988, he mobilized what he describes as the largest gathering of Messianic Jews in Israel in over 1,900 years—an event called Shavuot '88.

Sid preaching at a New Age festival in Israel: Once bound by the occult himself, Sid brings seekers of the counterfeit supernatural the real thing.

Sid leading an outreach in Israel.

Sid in Israel leading a "Lectures on the Supernatural" outreach.

Sid again ministering in Israel, reflecting a lifelong passion to see Jewish people come to faith in Yeshua.

During an outreach in Israel, this photograph captured what many believed reflected the tangible Glory of God resting on Sid as he ministered. Those present never forgot the extraordinary Presence of God they experienced that day.

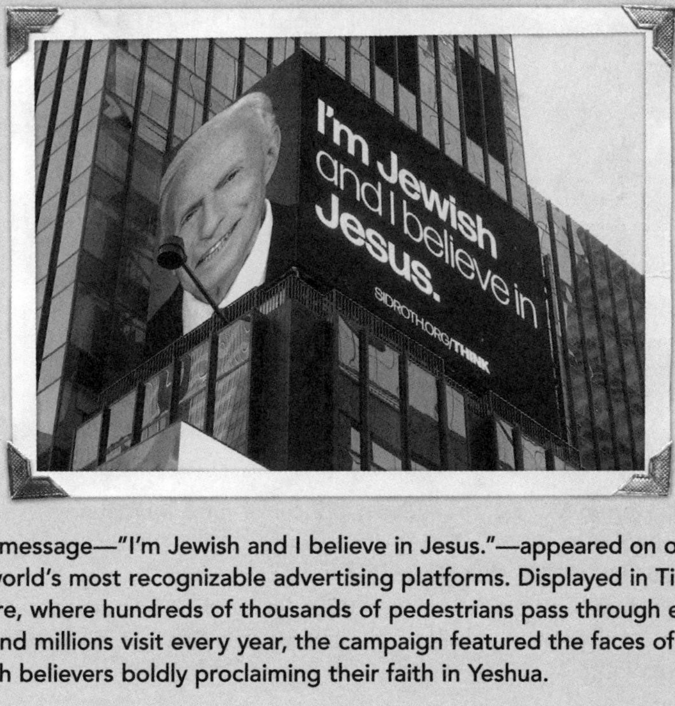

Sid's message—"I'm Jewish and I believe in Jesus."—appeared on one of the world's most recognizable advertising platforms. Displayed in Times Square, where hundreds of thousands of pedestrians pass through each day and millions visit every year, the campaign featured the faces of Jewish believers boldly proclaiming their faith in Yeshua.

Sid in the *It's Supernatural!* studio: He launched the weekly television program in 1996 with a straightforward plan. Each episode would feature testimonies of supernatural healings, dreams and visions, near-death experiences, and angelic encounters. The show was designed from the outset to reach Jewish people.

Sid with Warren Marcus, executive producer of *It's Supernatural!*: Warren had worked as an award-winning producer for *The 700 Club* and shared Sid's heart for Jewish evangelism. Sid writes that God directed Warren to join his team and teach him everything he needed to know about producing television, and helped him transform a God-given vision into a global platform.

Sid in his studio filming *It's Supernatural!*

Sid with Rabbi Jonathan Bernis.

Sid Roth and Rabbi Jonathan Cahn on set for *The Trilogy*.

Sid Roth was presented by Darren Canning with a prophetic painting he called *The Angel of Change*, inspired by what he sensed God was doing here. Today, that painting hangs in Sid's office as a constant reminder that God is always moving, guiding, and preparing His people for what comes next. Through every season of change, it reminds us to trust God's timing, embrace His leading, and remain expectant for the Greater Glory that lies ahead.

This picture shows the aftermath of a missile attack that hit our bomb shelter, one of three hundred bomb shelters Messianic Vision has built throughout Israel to date. Amazingly, the METV sign stayed upright.

More than fifty years after his encounter with God, Sid continues proclaiming Yeshua as Messiah and calling people to experience the supernatural reality of God for themselves.

ACT 6—THE FUTURE

At age eighty-five, Sid Roth continues proclaiming Yeshua as Messiah and inviting people to encounter the God who transformed his own life. Here, Sid is speaking at an outreach in Fort Lauderdale, Florida, at the Temple Aron HaKodesh in 2026. The rabbis at this congregation said there were *more* prebelieving (unbelieving) Jewish people at this single event than they had seen in many years combined. Healings and salvation occurred as a next level of Glory entered the room.

NOTES

Chapter 2

1. McCandlish Phillips, *The Bible, the Supernatural, and the Jews* (World Publishing Co., 1970).
2. Phillips, *The Bible, the Supernatural, and the Jews.*

Chapter 10

1. "Magda and André Trocmé in the Archives," International House, January 26, 2022, https://www.ihouse-nyc.org/magda-and-andre-trocme-in-the-archives/.
2. Martin Luther King Jr., "A Conversation with Dr. Martin Luther King, Jr.," in *Proceedings of the Rabbinical Assembly* (1968), Jewish Virtual Library, accessed May 4, 2026, https://www.jewishvirtuallibrary.org/martin-luther-king-on-israel-s-security.
3. Dr. Sol Lizerbram, "MLK: A Zionist Who Spoke Truth to Israel's Detractors," Jewish National Fund USA, accessed May 4, 2026, https://www.jnf.org/jnf-blog/jnf-wire/jnf-wire-stories/mlk-a-zionist-who-spoke-truth-to-israels-detractors.
4. Derek Prince, *Prophetic Destinies* (Creation House, 1992), 13.
5. Sid Roth, *Time Is Running Short* (Destiny Image Publishers, 1990), foreword.

Chapter 13

1. "46% of Adults Worldwide Hold Significant Antisemitic Beliefs, ADL Poll Finds," ADL, January 14, 2025, https://www.adl.org/resources/press-release/46-adults-worldwide-hold-significant-antisemitic-beliefs-adl-poll-finds.

2. Edward Helmore, "US Envoy Mike Huckabee Says It Would Be 'Fine' If Israel Took All Middle East Land," *The Guardian*, February 20, 2026, https://www.theguardian.com/us-news/2026/feb/20/mike-huckabee-israel-middle-east-tucker-carlson.

Chapter 14

1. Bible Hub, "*ishon*," accessed May 12, 2026, https://biblehub.com/hebrew/380.htm#google_vignette.

Chapter 17

1. Sid Roth's It's Supernatural!, "I Live in Israel. Here's What The Media Isn't Telling You," YouTube, March 10, 2026, https://www.youtube.com/watch?v=IjO7nOC3ZgI.

ABOUT THE AUTHOR

For more than five decades, Sid Roth has carried a singular and uncompromising vision: to proclaim that Jesus—Yeshua—is the Jewish Messiah, and that the supernatural promises of the Bible are real today.

A Jewish believer, media pioneer, author, and global evangelist, Sid Roth has spent his life standing at the intersection of Israel, the supernatural, and the manifest Presence of God—awakening millions to experiential faith.

Through television, radio, books, and worldwide media outreach, Sid has become one of the most recognizable voices exploring miracles, healing, prophetic revelation, and encounters with God. Yet behind the international ministry is a deeply personal story of searching, supernatural intervention, and radical transformation.

Born into a traditional Jewish family, Sid grew up proud of his Jewish identity but disconnected from religion. By age twenty-nine, he had achieved professional success as an account executive with Merrill Lynch, but inwardly he wrestled with a growing emptiness that success could not satisfy.

His search for meaning led him into Eastern meditation and New Age practices—only to leave him increasingly fearful and spiritually unsettled.

Everything changed when a Christian businessman challenged Sid with an unexpected idea: that the Hebrew

Scriptures pointed directly to Jesus as Israel's promised Messiah.

Determined to investigate for himself, Sid began reading the Jewish Scriptures and discovered something he had never been taught—that faith in Yeshua did not abandon Jewish identity but fulfilled it.

During one of the darkest moments of his search, overwhelmed and desperate, Sid prayed a simple prayer: "Jesus, help."

The next morning, the fear and torment that had gripped him were gone, replaced by a peace and love he had never known.

That encounter transformed his life.

God restored his family, renewed his purpose, and ignited a calling that would shape the next fifty years of his life.

Since 1972, Sid has devoted himself to one central mission: telling Jewish people—and the world—that Jesus is the Messiah and that God is still supernatural.

In 1977, that calling gave birth to *Messianic Vision*, founded upon the biblical mandate of Romans 1:16: "To the Jew first and also to the Gentile."

He believes that when Jewish people encounter their Messiah, it releases blessing and spiritual awakening that reaches far beyond one community and impacts the world.

That vision expanded nationally through *Messianic Vision* radio and globally in 1996 with the launch of *Sid Roth's It's Supernatural!*—the groundbreaking television program dedicated to documenting the reality of God through testimonies of healing, prophecy, deliverance, and transformed lives.

Unlike traditional religious programming, Sid's approach has always been marked by holy curiosity and bold expectancy. He investigates what many dismiss and asks the questions others avoid—always with one goal: to demonstrate that God is not distant and that the supernatural reveals His love and reality.

Today *It's Supernatural!* reaches audiences worldwide through television and digital media, while the It's Supernatural! Network (ISN) and Middle East Television (METV) extend that mission globally.

Yet despite decades of growth and influence, Sid's message has never changed.

Through more than thirty books, thousands of interviews, and countless ministry outreaches, one theme has remained central: the Glory of God—the manifest Presence of God that heals, restores, and reveals Jesus as living and real.

More than a broadcaster, author, or investigator of the supernatural, Sid Roth remains what he has always been: a Jewish man who encountered his Messiah and has spent the rest of his life making that reality impossible to ignore.

His message is simple.

God is real. Jesus is the Jewish Messiah. And the supernatural life found in Scripture is available today.

For Sid Roth, the greatest miracle has never been healing or supernatural signs.

It has always been the transforming power of meeting Yeshua, the Messiah of Israel.